Mythos Berlin
a London Perspective

A project by Sarah Hegenbart & Sven Mündner.
Edited in collaboration with Benjamin Eastham
Published alongside an exhibition of the same title, October 2012
Supported by the German Embassy London

Contents

Introduction
Sarah Hegenbart and Sven Mündner

The mythical status of Berlin is based on the fact that you have to fight with very few limitations. A lot is possible here. To feel free is very attractive and erotic. – Christian Boros

Looking at the crack in the purple oil paint on the canvas, we agreed that it was an integral part of the work. It had been added on the 6.05am Ryanair flight from Schönefeld to London Stansted when the canvas was rolled up in the overhead locker. The unplanned addition to the painting occurred roughly a year since the artist had decided to follow the call of Berlin, the city to which so many of his artist friends had recently moved. He was back in London to bring the painting to an exhibition at which he hoped it might be sold. Money too short for shipping, he simply de-stretched the canvas, rolled it up and brought it over as hand luggage. The work, and its accidental finish, struck us as a neat expression of the cultural relationship between London and Berlin which was fuelled by the advent of budget flights in the early Nineties.

Looking at this cracked paintwork was the start of a deeper investigation into why so many young people move to Berlin to live and work. There is no simple and singular explanation, so we labelled the phenomenon the *Mythos Berlin*, the legendary reputation that has proved so irresistible to a generation of artists, musicians and writers.

We ourselves were subject to the pull of Berlin. We arrived as naïve school leavers from the western provinces of Germany in the early 2000s. Before us, a daring generation had unearthed hidden bunkers and derelict basements for nightclubs, explored the charm of the city's eastern districts and created cultural phenomena like the Love Parade.

Introduction

In 2005 we left for London, part of a new wave of cultural migrants who flow in and out of Berlin.

Living in London, we were struck by people's excitement about Berlin. We were asked about this 'cool' place with its seductive 'cheap rents', 'parties in hidden basements' and 'vast studio space'. We were amazed at everyone's focus on the positive aspects of a complex city. This was the *mythos* surrounding Berlin. We almost didn't recognise the city from the descriptions we heard.

Berlin is very self-aware and self-conscious. Its cultural discourse is dominated by endless debate about itself. Its inhabitants are continually evaluating the city's standing, its advantages and disadvantages. Berliners are forever debating what the city is, and what it should be or should not be. In order to live the Berlin life it seems one has to develop a personal narrative precisely aligned with the city's cultural codex, as its population crafts narratives about Berlin to which the city is expected to conform. The most famous single statement of identity is perhaps Mayor Klaus Wowereit's phrase, uttered in an interview with the German magazine *FOCUS-Money* in 2003, that Berlin is 'poor but sexy'. The sense is of a place fluctuating between hyper self-awareness and daydreaming: myth-making in action.[1]

The OED defines *mythos* as 'a traditional or recurrent narrative scheme or plot structure'. According to Jan Assmann's functionalist concept of myths we might identify Berlin as a hot society that makes use of the power of the mythical structures to build and foster identities, provides an everyday code of conduct and helps to explain our environment. All three of the listed functions are apparent in Berlin's on-going conversation with itself.

The challenge of *mythos*, as Ernst Cassirer describes it, is that it is non-theoretical. Hence, a purely rational approach would not be a helpful tool when exploring the *mythos* surrounding Berlin. For this reason we have strived with this publication to present a variety of voices. The selection of texts was driven by conversations with authors and artists and is dominated by perspectives from the art world, a driving force in the city's cultural development. By including overlapping accounts or contradicting tales we hope to find key narratives that contribute to the construction of the *Mythos Berlin*, which might even be traced back, as one contribution suggests, to the Berlin of the Roaring Twenties.

Cassirer suggests that 'analysis of a mythos may proceed in a double direction. It may apply an objective or subjective method. In the former case it will try to classify the objects of mythical thought; in the latter it will try to classify its motives.'[2] In order to capture the many subjective narratives that collectively constitute the *Mythos Berlin* we were keen to document individual voices through interviews, essays and lyrical texts. We hope to obtain a degree of objectivity from the fact that we are viewing the *mythos* from the safe distance of London, and by including contributions from a variety of backgrounds including collectors, artists and curators both émigré and resident in London and Berlin.

Any attempt to comprehensively document the *mythos* surrounding Berlin is a mammoth project, and by focussing on the art world we have only skirted the periphery. We believe that the exercise is worthwhile nonetheless as an attempt to understand the cultural relationship between London and Berlin and as a means of documenting attitudes to Berlin at a time of great change. We hope that this might serve as a starting point in a deeper investigation into the phenomenology of a city that, at the beginning of the twenty first century, instilled a feeling of 'freedom' in its residents and exerted an 'erotic attraction' upon so many young immigrants from London and elsewhere.

This publication is neither a deconstruction nor a blind celebration of this attraction. It is written in the hope that many more generations will continue to knit the yarn of the *Mythos Berlin*.

1 Wunenberger, Jean-Jacques, 'Mytho-phorie. Formes et transformations du mythe' in *Religiologiques 10* (1994)
2 Cassirer, Ernst, *Essay on Man: An Introduction to a Philosophy of Human Culture.* (New Haven: Yale University Press, 1944)

Berlin Story
Rye Dag Holmboe

A drab June morning. The sky a uniform grey. The air filled with slow-falling rain. Tiny beads of moisture cling to his hair and trickle down his face. Clammy under his raincoat, he walks north west up Oranienburger Straße toward the U-Bahn, passing the reconstructed Neue Synagoge on his right, a Moorish affair whose Andalusian-coloured façade looks incongruous alongside the sober architecture that distinguishes this part of Mitte.

At an intersection the pavement has been torn up; two workmen in fluorescent vests stand smoking around a third, who clutches the handle of a jackhammer and guides its pulsating chisel in jagged lines. The air is rarefied by the sound of striking metal and dust. He watches as the tarmac cracks like a giant eggshell.

A little further along, at a safe distance from the deafening drill, he passes a row of bars and restaurants frequented by rowdy tourists, mostly British. These are the same revellers who will later solicit the services of the jaded street walkers who saunter along the pavement at night, their long legs on run-down heels, faces painted rose-white like synthetic angels. Hungry, he pauses, thumbs through the pages of a spiral bound menu, turns up his collar and continues, briskly.

After two hundred yards or so he notices a vast, dilapidated building on the other side of street. The front of the building is arched, its face covered in graffiti and pockmarked by broken windows, some of which have been boarded up, others left gaping. Stencilled across the façade is the word TACHELES, each white letter printed above one of the building's seven spandrels.

He crosses the street to take a closer look. For a moment the sun bursts through the clouds and splashes on the tarmac.

Berlin Story

Dazzled he is almost knocked over by a dreadlocked cyclist who clutches a bottle of beer under his arm. The man slurs an insult as he zigzags into the distance, a thin spray of water rising from his rear tire in a glittering ark.

A little vexed he makes his way to the building's entrance. Outside its portico two Turks sit on a brick wall. He guesses by the roundness of their faces and their almond-shaped eyes that they are brothers. The eldest, his dark hair gelled backwards, fiddles absent-mindedly with a pair of nail clippers; in his detachment there is something of the submissive female. The younger brother, a tattered bowler hat set back from his forehead, holds an umbrella with his right hand and sits on his left, his languid eyes gazing ahead at nothing in particular. As he walks past them an innate shyness causes him to feign abstraction and bite his bottom lip, but neither pays any attention to him.

The building's entrance is dimly lit, its walls covered in layers upon layers of peeling posters and graffiti. Not an inch has been left uncovered. The whole thing gives the impression of washed-out psychedelia. Each layer of the palimpsest adds to the gloomy stillness. The anarchist symbol is everywhere, as are anti-capitalist and apocalyptic slogans, many of which have been misspelled. He wonders whether this is deliberate, like the strange phonetic spelling sometimes encountered in the work of the Dadas.

His thoughts are interrupted by a grunt. To his right, hidden in the shadows, sits a hunchbacked figure with a flat face, a watering, loose-lipped mouth, the nose turned inwards, eyes bulging. The figure gestures with a diminutive forearm towards a donation box on the ground. Uneasy under the hunchback's gaze he feels a kind of moral discomfort.

He digs around in his pockets and, to his regret, pulls out a two euro coin. He doesn't dare to find another and throws it into the box.

He climbs up a dark flight of stairs to the first floor. Here he finds several empty artists' studios and what looks like the remnants of an installation. In a nave-like auditorium, whose red walls remind him of the insides of a yawning mouth, are the vestiges of some kind of apocalyptic drama. A human figure made of ragged cloth painted in swathes of black and pink has been hung over a railing. Another, arms outstretched, is being violated by a white demon. Both are watched over by a third figure, an impoverished mannequin made of thin bits of wood and string who stands demurely before a makeshift tripod as if to photograph the event. The air bristles with the sinister silence he imagines follows great catastrophes.

Leaving the auditorium he climbs a second flight of stairs and stops at the landing. Spray-paint covers a panelled window and prevents him from seeing out, though pale light trickles in, diffracted through layers of dark purple, burnt orange and bottle green. He passes his hand in front of it and lets the faint, swampy colours swirl on his skin. Through a broken windowpane his eye is drawn to a vacant lot down below full of odds and ends and bric-a-brac. In the lower left-hand corner stand massive sculptures made of scrap metal and bits of trash. Half-man half-machine they stand in attitudes of puzzled wonder, like uncouth monsters from out of the future. A rusty future.

Upstairs he is met by the stink of urine and the damp, fetid odour of a mildewed mattress. Turning a corner he finds himself enveloped in the yellowish light of a bulb that dangles from the ceiling in a halo of smoke. Empty beer bottles, plastic cups and fag butts litter the ground. The floor, slippery with garbage, glistens like glue. The whole room feels saturated with decay.

Sat on an old settee is a young man dressed in a makeshift pirate's costume. The soiled cuffs of his shirt stick out of a tattered, gold-buttoned admiral's jacket, his bellowing pantaloons are tucked into old knee-high patent leather boots and a pirate's hat sits atop a greasy tangle of black, oily hair. Between yellowing fingers he holds an unlit joint. His face is painted chalk-white. Sweat and grease have marked its surface with grey ravines. In their depths he sees misfortune, ennui, grief, suicide.

The man senses his gaze and fixes him with his hard dulled eyes. He stands up. Unsteady on his feet from too much drink, he murmurs something, then begins to speak. His voice is scraping. 'We're all dead, or dying, or about to die,' he says with an air of weariness. 'There will be no tomorrow, there is only this room, this day, only now.'

There is nothing else to get out of him. He rushes down the stairs and out into the flat grey light of mid-morning. Thunder threatens a storm. He turns up his collar and walks on.

Note from the editors: On 4 September 2012, when this publication was about to go to press, the Tacheles was finally shut down and the last 40 or so resident artists left the building.

Interview with Christian Boros

Sarah Hegenbart and Sven Mündner
Translated by Henrike Dessaules

18–26

SARAH HEGENBART

You get around a lot; you go to art fairs all over the world; you know artists in many different cities... In your opinion, how is Berlin different from other art capitals? What makes Berlin different from London, New York or Paris?

CHRISTIAN BOROS

Whenever I go to Paris, London and New York and tell people I come from Berlin, I always notice their eyes start gleaming. It is really quite confusing, because I am fascinated by these three cities: I find them exciting and wonderful and yet I am envied because I come from Berlin. I definitely think that Berlin is glorified, internationally. Everyone in the art scene dreams of Berlin, and I believe this fascination is founded in various different things, there's not a single cause. If it were just that Berlin was cheap, it wouldn't be enough to bring forth this fascination. There always have to be multiple reasons coming together, like a secret recipe, in order to fascinate: Wuppertal is cheap too. It does not explain the fascination of Berlin.

SARAH HEGENBART

What are the other reasons? Would you say that it is attributable to Berlin's history, for example the Golden Twenties, another time that Berlin held this mythical status?

CHRISTIAN BOROS

Yes, I believe this 'secret recipe' consists first and foremost of history. A *genius loci* never loses its karma. Rome will always be strong, because it used to be strong. Berlin has a tradition, a mix of history and the fact that it is a capital city

Interview with Christian Boros

of a particular population size. And then there is this mix of imperfection and curiosity. The city's imperfection is central to the fascination it inspires. Cities like Paris, which are so perfect, have a wonderful building structure and so on and so forth... They are complete, society is organised, you know who belongs and who doesn't. Structures that are complete are never as fascinating, because you cannot shape them anymore: they are at the end of their development. Berlin is not at the end of its development; it is in the middle of the process. Berlin is finding itself. The structures of who belongs, who are the opinion leaders, these structures are not yet completed. This means that, even as a young person coming in, you have the chance and opportunity to become part of the relevant set, which is very difficult in Paris. In Hamburg you need to have lived there for three generations to be able to participate. Berlin, on the other hand, is still a city coming into being. There are possibilities to become part of the game.

SARAH HEGENBART

You mean this openness, this equality of opportunity, where everyone can participate.

CHRISTIAN BOROS

Berlin has these gaps that can still be occupied by artists. In cities such as London or New York that is a lot more difficult, because the relevant chairs are already occupied. Here there are still open spaces. Of course, there are also the cheap rent prices, and moreover, the cheap partying, the cheap going-out and drinking. I mean, artists don't want to sit in their studios all day and fight with the canvas.

They want to go out, they want to drink a beer and eat in company. I believe that people are even more interested in other people than they are in art. Berlin is a place where a social life is financially possible, even for someone who doesn't have a lot of money. You can join the drinking and eating without having to be invited.

SARAH HEGENBART

What are the defining qualities of Berlin, would you say?

CHRISTIAN BOROS

Openness and curiosity. In other cities, when you're getting to know someone, he will tell you everything that he is doing. In Berlin he listens to what you have to say. I experience this all the time: Berlin is very curious about strangers.

SARAH HEGENBART

Perhaps you could also tell us a little bit about how you discovered the bunker [which now houses the Boros collection] and about how much Berlin has changed since then. If you were to see the bunker for the first time tomorrow, would it even still be possible for you to build up your collection there, to transform it into such a great art space?

CHRISTIAN BOROS

There was a time in Berlin when you didn't have to look, you just found. There were so many buildings screaming for a makeover. I think that was before the great real estate hype, when international investors flocked into the city. During that decade Berlin wasn't taken very seriously, because it was just so cheap.

Interview with Christian Boros

It wasn't like I was searching for a bunker; I was merely looking for a space that used to have a different purpose. I didn't want to move my collection into a new building, but to a place with history. And there used to be plenty of those around here. I was offered former schools, hospitals, a rheumatism clinic, a swimming bath and a bunker. I think it is very exciting to show how art can transform spaces. I liked the idea of doing this in a bunker which had been used in so many different ways. It was a great experiment to try and see whether the art could handle the building.

SARAH HEGENBART

Especially considering the long history. I mean, the bunker is really a symbol for Berlin's history.

CHRISTIAN BOROS

The history of the GDR, the invasion of the Russians, and even the Nazis; there are traces of all phases of Berlin's most recent history here, so this building has a lot to do with both Berlin and Germany. In 1940 they still believed in the final victory and constructed a building appropriate for the proposed city of Germania. So it looks like a sacred castle: it reflected the utopia of expected victory, and the bunkers which could not be demolished were supposed to fit nicely into the majestic cityscape. During the war the building was bombed, which left plenty of wounds – a symbol of Berlin's defeat. Then it became a Russian prison for the Nazis. In the GDR, bananas from Cuba were stored here, and in the Nineties techno music was founded here, Wolfgang Tillmans took his first pictures here... The bunker represents every phase that Berlin has experienced since 1940.

SVEN MÜNDNER
How has Berlin changed since the Nineties?

CHRISTIAN BOROS
A lot has changed since this used to be a techno bunker and part of the 'scene'. Thomas Scheibitz the painter and sculptor has lived only a couple of houses away from the bunker ever since the fall of the Wall. He says that this used to be borderland, a very tough area where you were not allowed to get close to the Wall without permission. It was no-man's-land. Then the Wall came down and this became the centre, the nucleus of the 'scene'. Nowadays I am in the tourist centre of Berlin. There are no more artists around here, only buses with tourists that get off and take pictures of the bunker. It has almost become an art-free zone, because this centre here, these few square kilometres, have become the most expensive area in all of Berlin. There are no more artists, only tourists.

SVEN MÜNDNER
Would you consider this a bad development and would you like to change that?

CHRISTIAN BOROS
No, I think that is simply the way it goes. It happens. You cannot turn this into an artificial island again, and build a wall to keep out those from Swabia and Wuppertal just because they increase bread, butter and rent prices. It is normal that things change and that there are phases in which things are cheap, then they get more expensive, then too expensive and finally it becomes uncool again. That's how cities change. I don't think we can talk about good or bad developments here.

Interview with Christian Boros

SARAH HEGENBART

Are you specifically interested in artists living in Berlin?
I am thinking of Anselm Reyle, Olafur Eliasson, Wolfgang
Tillmans...

CHRISTIAN BOROS

Absolutely! I am currently collecting Klara Liden's work, for
example. It's so much easier to meet up if someone lives in
Berlin. On Monday I met Wolfgang Tillmans, yesterday it was
Thomas Scheibitz, next week Klara Liden. You get together
for a glass of wine and some cheese, and that makes collecting easier, because you can have a chat without making big
arrangements or flying anywhere. You just meet up. That's
great!

SARAH HEGENBART

It allows you to discuss the work with the artists more inten-
sely, I suppose. Have you noticed any particular changes
recently, with regards to artists moving in the city? Or any
new trends in artists' practice? For example, performance art
is a big topic in London these days.

CHRISTIAN BOROS

Well, Berlin stays exciting. Someone from London or Paris
will hardly notice that artists move around in Berlin; that they
move from Mitte or Kreuzberg to Neukölln and Wedding. In
Berlin you always feel like everything changes, but the artists
stay in Berlin, and that certain areas get more expensive or
that people move, that's quite normal, I believe. It's a Berlin
view, to think that everything changes. But internationally
Berlin has been a centre for art production for a long time

and will continue to be so, because there are still hundreds and thousands of square metres of space. I believe Berlin will continue to bring forth great art for many, many more years. That is one answer to your question. The other answer: ten to fifteen years ago there was a trend towards making large work. Franz Ackermann used to paint on 3 × 3 m canvasses; Olafur Eliasson made large installations in gigantic studios with fifty assistants; Anselm Reyle with forty. The most recent exciting confrontations I had with art were in smaller studios with smaller works and sparse materials. Last night I talked to Dirk Bell about a work that is just 15 × 20 cm, highly concentrated. I think that the materials and the aesthetics will become more sparse and demure.

SARAH HEGENBART

I remember visiting Anselm Reyle's studio and he employed so many people – he even had someone searching on eBay for interesting objects to use in his work. The artists had become the supervisors to their assistants. What you mentioned sounds like a return to more traditional means of production.

CHRISTIAN BOROS

I think it has something to do with the financial crisis as well, and that studios have become more expensive and artists can't afford the big ones. That's a normal development, too.

SVEN MÜNDNER

How do you explain the near-mythical status that Berlin exerts on contemporary art practice?

Interview with Christian Boros

CHRISTIAN BOROS

The mythical status of Berlin is based on the fact that you have to fight with very few limitations. A lot is possible here. To feel free is very attractive and erotic. On top of that, the city is bursting with artists. The artists are connected: they don't work in solitude but in conversation with each other. They know each other and that creates a very healthy competitive atmosphere in which they stimulate each other. I know artists who work in complete solitude somewhere in Denmark; that is a completely different production process to here. When you meet each other at King Size on the dance floor or at a bar somewhere in Kreuzberg – this healthy rivalry and competition sparks off the production. The fact that Berlin is still developing means that there are still a lot of possibilities for participation here.

SARAH HEGENBART

Which means the myth can be made anew constantly. In London we are still talking about the YBAs, even though that was such a long time ago. That myth is so outdated, whereas in Berlin the myth is constantly being reanimated and enriched with new aspects. That is what keeps it so alive.

CHRISTIAN BOROS

Yes, you're right. I started buying art in London after the Freeze exhibition by Damien Hirst. I met Sarah Lucas and Tracey Emin and Marc Quinn, but it was a very short time. It was a brief window – there was a lot of poverty, unemployment and fatalism in London, when the artists came. Everything popped up very quickly, and then the chapter was closed. It's different in Berlin, because Berlin is still in the process and not completed yet. Cities are considered dead and boring for art production only when they are completed, and that's still far off. The myth is still being created here.

SARAH HEGENBART
Is there an art work that captures this Berlin spirit for you?

CHRISTIAN BOROS
I think the work of Manfred Pernice really reflects Berlin's patchwork, crafty and process-like state. His work deals a lot with architecture; his cans and blocks reflect what is often called the *Verdosung* ['containerisation'] of society.

SARAH HEGENBART
A last question: What do you consider will be the next 'mythical' city or art capital to replace Berlin?

CHRISTIAN BOROS
Complement. Not replace, but complement. Istanbul and Warsaw, I think.

Interview with Christian Boros

Arriving in the Present
Hannah Arnold

28 – 34

Cities are complex, endlessly fascinating phenomena. Even as simple a question as: 'What is a city?' triggers an endless cascade of new questions. In 1929, the German writer Martin Kessel expressed the opinion that any city could be thought of as being an ever-changing mythology. This statement seems to imply why a city's identity, like truth, is rarely pure and never simple: since a myth is a narrative which has been invented to justify or explain certain elements of human life – or in other words, a way of exerting power through the promotion of certain views – and since every city-dweller's myth about his city will vary from his neighbour's (as will his own, from time to time), a city can never have a singular, objective identity. She has to live with the identities which are ascribed to her by her inhabitants. A city knows who she is, but she has no voice.

In 1964, nearly twenty years after the fall of the Third Reich, the Austrian writer Ingeborg Bachmann presented her acceptance speech for the prestigious Büchner Preis to the Deutsche Akademie für Sprache und Dichtung. A slightly extended version of this text – which she began after moving to Berlin for a Ford Foundation residency in the wake of her traumatic break-up with Max Frisch – was published as *Ein Ort für Zufälle* ('A place for coincidences') in 1965. Both title and text are highly allusive. The primary meaning of the word *Zufälle* (literally: something which falls onto someone) becomes secondary in Bachmann's text as she adopts Georg Büchner's use of it in his disturbing novella Lenz, describing the bouts of madness from which its main character suffers. *Lenz*, a writer by profession, has left his home to escape the *weltschmerz* which torments him. In the mountains, he finds shelter with a parish priest who does his best to provide him with a stable living environment. But Lenz cannot escape his depression: 'The nightly *Zufälle* increased most terribly.'[1] It is crucial to note that Büchner does not present the *Zufälle* as the result of Lenz's madness, but as something originating in the external world which haunts the sensitive artist and which he cannot escape: 'It was as if something followed him, as if something horrendous was trying to reach him, something which humans could not stand the sight of, as if insanity was chasing him on horseback.'[2] This fatalist view fascinated Bachmann; she adopted it to describe a certain uncanny *etwas* (something) which, she felt, had become an intrinsic part of Berlin:

> *Madness can come from the outside as well, towards the individual, has thus moved to the outside – at a much earlier point of time – from the insides of the individuals, heads back now, in situations which have become familiar to us, in the heritages of this time.*[3]

To Bachmann, the emotional imbalance which she sensed in Berlin was a direct consequence of the city's traumatic historical heritage. She thought of the general lack of intellectual engagement with this heritage as a medical condition: a state of drowsiness and disease. Her disturbing text, therefore, was meant to cure her German contemporaries from their *Zufall*-induced slumber and self-denial, by forcing them to acknowledge the past and to revive repressed memories. Bachmann's aim was to support the growth of a discourse which was only emerging as late as the mid-sixties, triggered for instance by the 'Auschwitz Prozess' (1963 – 1965) and by the increasing activism of left-wing groups and communes. In the midst of this intense and claustrophobic transition period, Bachmann consciously adopted both the role and perspective of the (Austrian) outsider, both in Berlin and in *Ein Ort für Zufälle*.

While one cannot help feeling that, at least to a degree, Bachmann might have been projecting her own unstable state of mind on her environment, her criticism was justified. Only two years prior to her arrival in Berlin a visible rupture had appeared in its cityscape: the city Bachmann had moved to was a divided space where the flow of life was interrupted both physically and emotionally. This manifested itself in a monument that would quickly come to symbolise the divided state of the western world. No wonder that she could not help making a link between *Lenz* and Berlin: 'The world... had a monstrous rupture'.[4] Bachmann interpreted the division of Germany as a facet of that repression of past which she was criticising.

Berlin, however, was busy enough struggling with its present identity: as *Frontstadt*, as the capital of a schismatic world, the space in which the clash of two opposing ideologies was tangible. Berlin had not yet been given time to pause, to breathe freely and reflect on the *Zufälle* which it had experienced and was still experiencing. Until the fall of the Wall – when the segregated energy of a divided nation was suddenly released, allowed to reunite, and finally available for the fuelling of national reflection – Berlin was in a state of shock, its identity schizophrenic. This made it nearly impossible to write about the situation without taking sides. Bachmann, the outsider, created a text about the city in which her projection of personal trauma and the detection of general trauma mixed; a mingling of the subjective and the objective. While her picture of Berlin was certainly biased, its bias did not follow the unwritten rules of the

East-West divide. Bachmann herself pointed out that, instead, it was her experience of Austria's annexation by the Nazis during her childhood which shaped her views. In her acceptance speech, she stated: 'I urge you not to confuse what I will attempt to say with impressions. I might have impressions, but who will rely on those!'[5] Not impressed by Berlin, Bachmann was able to preserve that claustrophobia and silence in *Ein Ort für Zufälle* which haunted Germany during the sixties: the text can thus be read as a lyrical testimony to the post-war atmosphere by all those who didn't experience it first hand.

After the Wende in 1989, Germany had to undergo a process of complex readjustments. Berlin, delivered from her difficult double-role, was facing a personality crisis, an uncertain future but, at the same time, endless possibilities. In his paper 'The Voids of Berlin', published in 1997, Andreas Huyssen, Villard Professor of German and Comparative Literature at Columbia University, expressed his worries about the direction which the city's development might be taking:

> Part palimpsest, part Wunderblock, Berlin now finds itself in a frenzy
> of future projections and, in line with the general memorial obsessions
> of the 1990s, in the midst of equally intense debates about how to negotiate
> its Nazi and communist pasts now that the safe dichotomies of the cold war
> have vanished.[6]

While Germany's dichotomous identity during the previous decades – a black-and-white picture painted by the two opposing political systems which defined themselves primarily as being non-Other – provided both East and West with a relatively stable frame of self-reference, its reunification made it necessary for the country to re-define and re-invent herself. Freedom came with choice, choice with responsibility, and thus finally the spell was broken: Germany's thorough, unanimous engagement with her fascist and communist pasts became inevitable. In this as in most other respects, Berlin remained the nation's figurehead: the public as well as the academic interest in her future was immense. At the time, Huyssen wrote pessimistically that 'Berlin may be the place to study how this new emphasis on the city as cultural sign, combined with its role as capital and the pressures of large-scale developments, prevents creative alternatives and thus represents a false start into the twenty-first century. Berlin may be well on the way to squandering a unique chance.'[7] With such a traumatic past and yet so many voids to be filled, he feared that she might cut lack for self-confidence, choose the wrong role-models and become as flashy and commercial as he considered New York to be.

But Berlin took a different route: having dispersed the *Zufälle* by finally engaging with her past, she was convalescing quickly. Instead of adorning herself with bright lights or trying hard to conjure up her pre-WWII identity as 'Chicago an der Spree', Berlin became a place for *Einfälle* (ideas). During the past twenty years, the city's reputation in the world has changed immensely: from the scarred, divided and unsettled victim of Third Reich and Cold War politics to an iconic, vibrant, and artistic metropolis. In Berlin, the infamous 'Berlinerluft' seems oversaturated with creativity, the night-life peaks only at 5am, and life seems incredibly cheap. It is the place where, in the past decades, alternative culture has been celebrated so much that the urge to be different appears to have become a mainstream phenomenon:

Arriving in the Present

strict dualism has sprouted into diversity. Most cultural institutions, for example, exist more than once: an ironic consequence of the city's decade-long division. And since reunification, much time and money has been invested in filling the city's physical voids with architecture that looks both backwards and forwards. As a result of all this effort, today's (artistic) visitors to Berlin – unlike Ingeborg Bachmann – seem impressed by what the city has to offer.

Berlin's growing integrity and charm has had and will continue to have an impact on the way in which the city is perceived. Young tourists from around the globe, who already trail the city en masse, might not primarily be interested in museums like Topographie des Terrors but they might well be telling their friends at home about Tacheles, the heart of Berlin's alternative art scene, located in a ruined building at Oranienburger Straße which has been occupied by artists since 1990. While of course signs of the past continue to be omnipresent throughout the city, Berlin's identity (as much as any other place's) is primarily dependent on and formed in the mind of the beholder: those who do not allow their perception to be shaped by personal experiences, background reading, historical knowledge, or a conscious effort to detect traces of the past in the cityscape will experience a very different city than those who do.

With its ever-growing number of foreign visitors and inhabitants, Berlin must adapt to and assume the identity imposed upon it: a creative hub; a place for Einfälle rather than an inhabited memorial and museum, perpetually reminding its citizens of the necessity of remembrance. Even for those native Germans who, like myself, were born around the time of reunification (and are beginning to shape the undivided country into which we were born!), the division of Germany feels like a rather abstract concept. When I picture a fragmented Germany, for instance, I think of a division into regions, rather than its former division into halves. Similarly, in Berlin, the city's present is more real to me than its turbulent past. This is not to suggest that younger generations are ignorant of twentieth century history but rather that Berlin is finally arriving in the present, exactly because it is so young and international and creative. Its quasi-mythical status in the world corresponds with a deeper truth; Bachmann was right: 'Es ist etwas in Berlin'. There is! Only her mysterious, uncanny and negative *etwas* has shifted shape: it has become positive, unrestrained, productive and social.

---

1   'Die Zufälle des Nachts steigerten sich auf's Schrecklichste'
2   'Es war als ginge ihm was nach, und als müsse ihn was Entsetzliches erreichen, etwas das Menschen nicht ertragen können, als jage der Wahnsinn auf Rossen hinter ihm'
3   'Der Wahnsinn kann auch von außen kommen, auf die einzelnen zu, ist also schon viel früher von den Innen der einzelnen nach außen gegangen, tritt den Rückweg an, in Situationen, die uns geläufig geworden sind, in den Erbschaften dieser Zeit.'
4   'die Welt...hatte einen ungeheuren Riß'
5   'Verwechseln Sie, was ich zu sagen versuchen werde, nicht mit Eindrücken. Ich habe womöglich welche, aber wer wird sich auf Eindrücke verlassen!' Hans Höller, Ingeborg Bachmann: Das Werk. Von den frühesten Gedichten bis zum 'Todesarten' – Zyklus
6   Huyssen, 'The Voids of Berlin' *Critical Inquiry, Vol 24*, No. 1
7   *ibid.*

Bettina Pousttchi: Echo Berlin

Richard Cork

Although she lived in Mainz for the first nineteen years of her life, and subsequently moved to New York and Paris, Bettina Pousttchi has been settled in Berlin since 2005. Pousttchi first saw the Palast der Republik when visiting Berlin in the 1990s. Aware of its history as the former East German parliament from 1976 to 1990, she was also fascinated by the fact that it had been built on the site of the former Stadtschloss, the city castle gravely damaged during the Second World War and then demolished by the GDR government. Pousttchi soon realised that, 'during the GDR period, people in Berlin had mixed feelings about the Palast. It was a governmental structure of repression, but you could also have a good time there, visiting the glamorous restaurant, the bowling alley, dancing clubs and theatre. It was a *Volkshaus*, for the people.'

After Germany's reunification, the Palast 'became an iconic building for the new Berlin. And it raised an important questaion: can buildings be rehabilitated and tell another story? The Palast had a dark history, but the new Berlin also attempted to use this building in a new way. So there was over a decade of discussion about whether to destroy it. The big argument against preserving the Palast was asbestos, but it was mainly a problem of ideology. So eventually there was a government vote to demolish it, but only with a lot of opposition. It was cruel for people, of all kinds, to see their history obliterated. I couldn't believe it myself. It was quite a brutal situation, so in 2006 I felt the need to record the Palast before it was gone.'

During that summer, Pousttchi made videos and took photographs while the building was being demolished. 'You couldn't go in, so I only filmed the outside, but from all kinds of positions. I then started editing the images of this semi-destroyed building, but they didn't come together. The demolition took three years, and there were protest demonstrations. For certain people it had a beauty, and even for me the Palast had a very strange Eastern European modernist glamour. Half destroyed, it looked raw and brutal – really like a wound. And then, all of a sudden, there was nothing left except a green lawn. I remember feeling a huge void after the Palast disappeared, but I also felt that it was still there, like an after-image on your retina.'

Berlin wanted to reconstruct the former Stadtschloss, but then everyone realised just how much it would cost to build this replica of the old city castle. Even so, the Temporäre Kunsthalle was erected on a nearby site while the demolition of the Palast went ahead. 'This new building was conceived by the architect to have contemporary art on the façade as well as inside', explains Pousttchi, 'and they asked me to make a photographic proposal.' After a period of intense thought, she arrived at her highly adventurous decision to make an immense photographic interpretation of the Palast on the outside of the Temporäre Kunsthalle. 'I felt surprised and challenged rather than delighted with the idea', she recalls, admitting that 'I had a shock when I realised the building was 57 metres deep, 20 metres wide and 11 metres high. I was like: "Oh, my god, I've only got two months to do this!"'

At first, she tried to use her own photographs of the Palast, but they had all been taken during the destruction of the building. 'So then I tried to find other material, and looked through the archives.' In the end, Pousttchi used scans from archival pictures of the Palast to create the 970 separate paper posters that, glued together, covered the entire façade of the Temporäre Kunsthalle. Her daring and determination paid off. 'I was overwhelmed by the public's response', she recalls with a sense of wonder. 'It started while I was installing. Everyone could take a picture, and I had all kinds of reaction from spectators, commentators and journalists. They were enthusiastic as well as critical, and people started telling me their memories. After all, I was dealing with their lives and a building that had gone. But they recognised *Echo* at once as the mirrored bronze façade of the Palast, even though it now had a completely different shape. The original building had a coat of arms in the middle, but it symbolised the GDR and I didn't want to bring it back. So I turned it into a clock, and some people became convinced that there had always been a clock on the façade of the Palast!'

After *Echo* was finished in 2009, Pousttchi spent a long time photographing it in situ. 'It was fascinating to see this fake façade in the context of Berlin', she says. 'I didn't want to evoke sadness, but memory and respect towards the past. The Palast was a part of Berlin's history which should not be erased, even if in bookshops you can hardly find a record of it today. Some people now even think that *Echo* was the Palast!' Working on such an ambitious project changed Pousttchi's attitude towards her own art. 'Looking back now, I realise it's where everything came together in my work. Photography and sculpture became architecture in a very special place. I'm more sensitive to locations now, and my major projects are site-specific. While I was photographing *Echo Berlin* [the title of the photographic series documenting the sculpture], I had sleepless nights about the posters peeling off. I also realised how vulnerable it was, and expected it to be graffiti-attacked. But I was very glad that there wasn't a single graffito, even though *Echo* had left the privileged and protected space of the museum far behind.' The potency of the work is conveyed with great intensity in Pousttchi's photographs, which in 2011 formed the centrepiece of her remarkable exhibition *Echo: Mirroring Memories*, organised by the German Embassy in London. Curated by Sarah Hegenbart, it was held in the German House at 34 Belgrave Square, the former Embassy of the GDR. Pousttchi was astonished when she discovered this unexpected piece of history. 'When Sarah told me it was once the GDR Embassy, I couldn't believe my ears', she recalls, 'because I never imagined GDR outside the borders of Germany. The state wasn't respected immediately, and not every country had a GDR Embassy.' So Pousttchi regarded 34 Belgrave Square as 'a very special location which added another layer of meaning to my *Echo Berlin* photographs. As I was looking for some trace of the building's history, the guards told me to look at the chairs in the cafeteria. They all had yellow labels printed with the words 'Property of the GDR', so the chairs were the last remaining trace of that period. I decided to make them part of my installation. They became sculpture, and my photographs of *Echo Berlin* ended up relating to their space in a site-specific way, which I thought was very exciting.'

Berlin Rent Prices and the Effects of Gentrification
Fact Sheet

42 – 44

Average European housing prices[1]

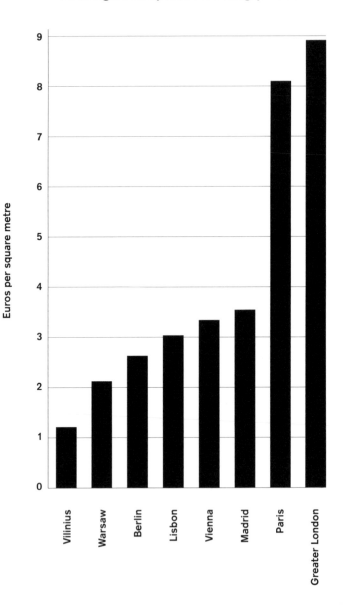

Euros per square metre

Vilinius · Warsaw · Berlin · Lisbon · Vienna · Madrid · Paris · Greater London

Berlin Rent Prices and the Effects of Gentrification

What is the one defining factor that makes Berlin so irresistible for artists, young entrepreneurs and students alike? Clearly, it is the well-known aspect of low living costs, especially cheap rent prices that are unprecedented in Western European capital cities.

Compared to London in particular, Berlin appears to be a freelance artists' paradise, with living costs up to three times lower than those of the British capital. Creative folks from all over the world are fleeing the neoliberalised Western metropolises that offer great economic opportunities for a few, and dismal living conditions for everyone else. Berlin, on the other hand, promises just the opposite. But what if these conditions were to change?

Gentrification and its effects, particularly higher rent prices, is currently the most passionately debated topic among the city's inhabitants. The steep increase in rent costs is no longer a rumour, but an undeniable reality. Projects such as 'Mediaspree' and the BMW Guggenheim Lab promise to upgrade fiercely contested public spaces and residential quarters. However, residents fear that they will only upgrade inequalities by encouraging investments in office spaces and townhouses for the upper middle class.

The position of artists in all of this is a little bit on the fence. On the one hand, they are seriously affected by the higher rents, due to their generally precarious work conditions and their specific needs for studio and exhibition spaces. Already, studio space is worryingly limited and the declining vacancy rate is hardly consistent with the increasing demand.

On the other hand, artists are also considered the avant-garde of any gentrification process, turning previously unattractive proletarian and immigrant neighbourhoods into hip communities for subcultures and the young urban elite. It is no coincidence that the majority of artists tend to live in the areas that have become the most desirable with the sharpest increase in rent prices.

Wrangelstraße, pictured in 2005, was one of the epicentres of a heated debate among residents about gentrification and rent increases.

This probably explains why, until recently, artists did not join the protests or speak out publicly, and they were harshly criticised for this complacency. The impending closure of the central art space Tacheles on Oranienburger Straße may have been the final wake-up call. Artists have come to realise that the reasons for why they came to Berlin in the first place may slowly disappear.

Written and researched by Henrike Dessaules

1   Sources compiled at *The Needle*, needleberlin.com

2   *Wohnmarkt Report 2012*, GSW Immobilien AG, Berlin 2012.

3   *Studio Berlin II,* Institut für Strategieentwicklung, June 2011.

4   *Wohnmarkt Report 2012*, GSW Immobilien AG, Berlin 2012.

Interview with Bettina Pousttchi

Sarah Hegenbart

Translated by Sarah Günther

Architecture is an important inspiration for your work. I am thinking here especially of *Echo* and *Framework*. Do you think architectural spaces in London could serve as an inspiration to you in the same way as Berlin's historical sites?

BETTINA POUSTTCHI

For some years I have been fixing photographic works onto the façades of buildings. *Echo*, on the façade of the Temporäre Kunsthalle Berlin referred to the Palast der Republik, which had just been demolished on that very spot. *Framework*, installed on the Schirn Art Gallery in Frankfurt, dealt with the redevelopment of the Old Town. The respective architecture does not necessarily have to be located in Germany. It can be situated anywhere. In 2010, for example, I installed my work *Basel Time* on the façade of the front building of Art Basel in Switzerland, which has since been demolished. Likewise, I am very interested in particular examples of architecture.

SARAH HEGENBART

Could you tell us a bit more about the work on *Echo*? How does it refer to Berlin's complex history?

BETTINA POUSTTCHI

Echo was a photo-installation, in which I completely covered the four outsides of the Temporäre Kunsthalle with 970 paper posters. The different posters created an all-round photographic scene that recalled the Palast. It wasn't a detailed replica of the vanished icon, but a photographic adaptation of it. For six months the photo-sculpture stood on Schlossplatz in the historical centre of Berlin, right next to the Cathedral, the Red City Hall and the Museum Island.

Between 2008 and 2010 the Temporäre Kunsthalle was put up as an exhibition venue on the Schlossplatz. Presentations took place both inside the gallery and on the outer façade of the building, which was made of plywood. In immediate proximity to the gallery the Palast der Republik had recently been demolished and suddenly there was a striking urban gap.

The Palast was a fascinating building. Built in the 1970s, it served as Parliament house of the German Democratic Republic but was also designed as an entertainment centre. Aside from parliamentary rooms, it contained a theatre, a bowling alley, a discotheque, restaurants and a concert hall.

After the fall of the Berlin wall and the dissolution of the Eastern German parliament the building lost its initial function. In the re-unified Germany it stood empty for a long time, but was still used as a venue for exhibitions and performances. After a long-standing political debate it was demolished. Right there, where the Palast had been standing before, the Berlin city palace is about to be built. The original building had been destroyed in World War II. *Echo* made reference to this process of urban planning.

SARAH HEGENBART
Tell us a bit more about the time you spent in London. How did living here affect your artistic practice?

BETTINA POUSTTCHI
In 2008 I visited London for six months to do a residency at TrAIN, the Research Centre for Transnational Art, Identity

and Nation. It was a fascinating and exciting period that I look back upon with joy. London is a world city, whereas Berlin is still a far cry from that. Because I could realise certain works only in Berlin, I travelled a lot between London and Berlin. The one hour time difference between such closely connected cities has always confused me and made me reconsider this ordering principle. It was one of the triggers for the photo series *World Time Clock*, where I am taking pictures of public clocks in different time zones.

SARAH HEGENBART

Which building in London could you imagine intergrating into your work?

BETTINA POUSTTCHI

London has a very interesting architectural history. There are many buildings that I would like to work with. I have always been interested in the traces of British industrial architecture.

SARAH HEGENBART

When did you move to Berlin? Why?

BETTINA POUSTTCHI

I was born in Germany and grew up there, most of the time. During my studies I have lived in various cities abroad and moved to Berlin in 2005. Berlin has become a very tolerant, open and international place. I enjoy living here.

SARAH HEGENBART

If you were at the beginning of your career today, would you feel compelled to live in Berlin?

Interview with Bettina Pousttchi

BETTINA POUSTTCHI

Berlin is changing a lot. Many open spaces get lost; many neighbourhoods are turned upside down. Nevertheless, I would move to Berlin again and again.

SARAH HEGENBART

Something that has arisen during our research for this book is the idea that the 'existential pressure' faced by artists in London can be inspiring. Do you agree with this?

BETTINA POUSTTCHI

When I finished school I moved to Paris to study there. That was in the early nineties. No matter how exciting Paris has been, I also experienced a lot of 'existential pressure' in this crowded, difficult and very expensive city. A pressure like that can motivate and encourage, but it can also inhibit and restrain. I think that good living and working conditions for artists have a more positive effect at the end of the day.

SARAH HEGENBART

How does living in Berlin feature in your work?

BETTINA POUSTTCHI

Many of my works have their point of departure in Berlin. For the photo series *Take Off* I took pictures of Tempelhof airport in 2005, just before it was closed down. The photo series *Parachutes* has its origins in an air show in Berlin. The sculptures of the *Squeezer* series, which were made of street posts, were named after Berlin streets. In my opinion, in Berlin the presence of history is so strong that you cannot ignore it when you live here.

SARAH HEGENBART

How would you describe the main differences between Berlin and London as art centres?

BETTINA POUSTTCHI

In contrast to London, the situation for institutions of contemporary art in Berlin is problematic. The existing institutions are under-resourced. A diverse art scene does not receive enough visibility. There has been a long fight to rectify this. The Temporäre Kunsthalle on Schlossplatz was one of many initiatives to achieve this.

SARAH HEGENBART

Where else could you imagine working if not in Berlin? Could you imagine coming back to London?

BETTINA POUSTTCHI

I really like living in Berlin and this is my base. The time in London was, however, fantastic and I would like to spend more time there.

Interview with Bettina Pousttchi

Colour Plates

52 – 53

Bettina Pousttchi
Echo Berlin (2009 – 2010)
Photographs, 115 × 165 cm
© Bettina Pousttchi, courtesy
Buchmann Galerie, Berlin

54 – 55

Olafur Eliasson
Berlin Colour Sphere (2006)
Boros Collection

56

Andreas Greine and Fabian Knecht
ENTLADUNG (2012)
Intervention in public space
Airport Berlin Tempelhof

57

Wolfgang Tillmans
outside Bunker (1992)
Maureen Paley, London: Galerie Buchhollz,
Cologne / Berlin: Andrea Rosen Gallery,
New York

58

Jost Münster
Anlage (2010)
Acrylic, wood, spray paint
74 × 35 × 8 cm

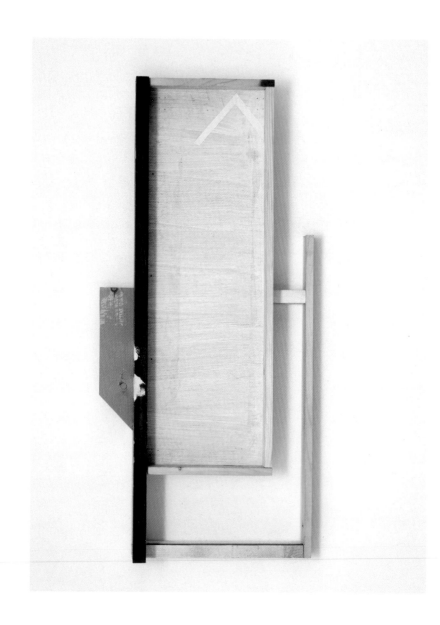

Berlin: An Old and New Promise

Aeneas Bastian

Translated by Henrike Dessaules

Understanding Berlin's image as one of the most vibrant centres for contemporary art in Europe today requires a familiarity with its turbulent history during the twentieth century.

Formerly associated with names such as Walter Gropius, Fritz Lang and George Grosz, Berlin's role as a cultural metropolis during the heyday of the Weimar Republic disappeared as the Nazi terror suffocated artistic freedoms and attempted to eliminate the great patrons and supporters of the arts. At the end of the Second World War, Berlin was nothing but rubble and debris. As reflected in Roberto Rossellini's 1948 film *Germania anno zero,* Berliners had to embark on a bitter path from oblivion.

The division of Berlin, cemented by the building of the Wall, was the most painful rupture in the city's history. In the post-war years, West Berlin was turned into a capitalist island on GDR territory; a window on the West. But the city's western section was on the brink when the US finally decided to supply people with the so-called *Rosinenbombern*, the planes that dropped supplies into Berlin during the blockade of the city by the USSR in 1948. John F. Kennedy's affirmation of the 'free world' culminated in a symbolic confession: 'Ich bin ein Berliner'.

Following the fall of the Wall, the two parts of the city lost their respective superior authorities: the Allied Forces and the former Soviet Union. Suddenly, Berlin was confronted with a new role, one that brought with it the unforeseen opportunity of becoming one of the liveliest cultural metropolises in Europe.

Although the economic consolidation of the new Berlin failed to materialise, artists and intellectuals made the most of the new era. Primarily due to the influx of a number of young artists starting in the early nineties, who came to live and work in undivided Berlin, the city underwent profound changes during the two decades after the *Wende,* the 'turning point' of reunification. These young artists turned Berlin into a key site for the production of contemporary art, meaning gallerists, curators and collectors were also drawn to the city. A witness to failed utopias and totalitarian systems, the city functioned remarkably well as a workplace for artists because it still offered the possibility for development. The influx of artists to the city can be explained by the possibilities for experimentation it offered. Flats and studios were affordable, even for less established artists. They were followed by small galleries and project spaces that spread rapidly in the new gallery area of Mitte, which quickly developed into the epicentre of the Berlin art scene. Contemporary Fine Arts and *neugerriemschneider* were among the emergent galleries, showing previously unheard of artists such as Daniel Richter, Jonathan Meese and Olafur Eliasson.

Renowned architects contrasted extraordinary individual constructions with the uniformity of Berlin's countless functional buildings designed according to technical standards and rarely in line with aesthetic principles. Frank Gehry's house at Pariser Platz is exemplary of these counterpoints, while the 'Museum Island' on the Spree was given a makeover by David Chipperfield's recreation of the New Museum and I.M. Pei's extension of the German Historical Museum.

Public institutions also changed rapidly at this time, complemented by exhibition spaces that emerged from private initiatives. The KunstWerke Institute for Contemporary Art, which gave rise to the first Berlin Biennale, established itself as a platform for the exhibition of diverse young contemporary art.

Berlin continued to lack the support of paramount private collectors and benefactors like Peter Ludwig, whose roots were in the Rhineland, despite regular collaborations with the state museums of the GDR. However, Berlin museums tried to compensate for this lack by permanently integrating singular private collections of modern and contemporary art into their repertoire. Erich Marx, lender of seminal works by Beuys, Twombly and Warhol, became a partner of the Hamburger Bahnhof, while Friedrich Christian Flick lent and even donated works by Flavin, Nauman and the late Franz West to the museum.

Heinz Berggruen, a Jewish art dealer born in Berlin in 1914, made a decisive gesture towards the historical reconciliation of Berlin as the capital of a reunified Germany. In 1996, he decided to make the German capital the home of his extraordinary collection, which including significant works by Picasso, Giacometti, Braque, Matisse and other iconic modern artists.

Berlin's image, its magnetic attraction to so many of today's artists, is probably the result of the historical ruptures and turning points that remain visible in its cityscape to this day. It is this incompletion and contradiction that lends the city its unique appeal. Berlin remains a place that tempts without proffering any certainties: a promise.

Berlin / London
Susanna Davies-Crook

'I'm going to be a great film star! That is, if booze and sex don't get me first' – Sally Bowles

Such is the immortal line uttered by Lisa Minelli's divinely decadent Sally Bowles in the 1972 film, *Cabaret*. It might, for the purposes of this essay, be quite possible to substitute the words 'booze and sex' for Berlin. Berlin 'getting you', one imagines, constitutes a dissolution into hedonism. London 'getting you', on the other hand, conjures up images of eviction for not being able to pay the rent and a spiral of despair upon not having 'made it'. Émigrés to Berlin, particularly those from business capitals, escape their respective cities for the exemption from a world of progress-driven narrative. Before I left London I visited an artist at their studio who was also heading to Berlin for the summer, to 'cycle around and think and drink coffee, because you can do that in Berlin'.

The tower on Memhardstraße in which I now sit was previously a Stasi officers' apartment block. Up here on the third floor, I look across to similar blocks. Beneath my feet lay several layers of soundproofing; the TV tower at Alexanderplatz is in my eyeline. All are reminders of the historical palimpsest of Berlin, and the importance of space to our understanding of the city.

Berlin, having survived the twentieth century's assault upon it, is a city attractive to romantics. It is somewhere that people come for experience, for the cabaret. It is a city that prioritises performance over academicism. Artists are moths to its flame, for practical as well as romantic reasons. If we take it as read that artists need space then the attraction of a city in which the cost of living is low and the quality of life high is obvious. Part time jobs in the service industry are

Berlin / London

enough to pay the rent, whereas in London a forty hour week on the minimum wage is barely enough to subsist.

Since the fall of the Wall much of Berlin has been up for grabs. Javier Peres, the art world *enfant terrible* who now runs two spaces in Berlin, tells me that 'I opened the [Peres Projects] gallery in Kreuzberg in 2005, and it just felt like you could do anything. Those first two or three years, up to 2008, we were doing anything and everything: these crazy parties, these crazy installations, huge spaces. Everything was possible in a way you can't even imagine. If you had to rent a venue for a night after an opening at the gallery you could rent a 1920s – era indoor swimming pool in Prenzlauer Berg for 500 euros. Can you imagine?'

A typical Sunday at Mauerpark in Prenzlauer Berg

This is perhaps the fundamental difference between creativity in Berlin and London. Where in London risk assessments take up more time than planning the show, and where artists live in constant fear of getting shut down by the council, in Berlin I've snuck into a grass verge by an underpass to watch a pop-up screening of David Cronenberg's *Crash* as cars rumble by overhead and tail-lights disappear into the distance; walked half an hour through the suburbs of Marzahn to a derelict apartment building to watch *Die Architekten*. At eight this evening I will meet a mixture of Germans and expats by an U-bahn to walk to a secret location where a film will be shown. We will likely have to clamber over obstacles to get in, the building will not be boarded up or sealed off, and we will not be wearing hard hats. There will be no red tape.

By contrast, London's own 'Secret Cinema' is a strictly regulated commercial operation that has lost much of the forbidden adrenaline rush of trespass. This is without even mentioning the many 'open airs' that take place in public parks in summer all over Berlin: pop-up actions, parades, festivals.

In Berlin, the city feels like she belongs to you and the people respond by setting up impromptu events, tables, building odd DIY vessels and setting them afloat on the canals with speakers teetering drunkenly atop. In London, you belong to her, public business takes place in private, and private space is fiercely guarded even when it lies empty – as the Oubliette art collective, notorious for squatting prominent empty buildings, would attest. South East London art spaces Auto Italia and Woodmill have both recently been demolished to make way for housing complexes; Hackney's James Taylor Gallery warehouse has also been closed down. Artists' spaces in London are considerably harder to find, and considerably harder to keep.

Berlin / London

The two cities are of course linked, by artistic preoccupations as much as Easyjet flight routes. Peckham might now be tenuously twinned with Neukölln, two off-centre districts with low rents and artistic communities. The expat artist community in Neukölln centres around Times, a bar run by artists Max Pitegoff and Calla Henkel, and there is a palpable sense of cross-pollination with London. Yuri Paterson, a founding member of the South East London art collective LuckyPDF, says that 'there is a growing relationship with Peckham and Berlin', which extends particularly to Berlin's thriving music scene. Music and art is in Berlin inseparable: the frequent 'hangings' of artwork at Times are popular more for the parties that bring together artists as a scene which stretches across New York, Amsterdam, London and Berlin.

Berlin retains its mythical status as the city in which to carouse because of these meeting points, deliberately promoted by the city mayor's deathless description of it as 'arm, aber sexy' [poor, but sexy]. Yet the fear that such commercialisation of Berlin's unique atmosphere, and rapidly increasing tourism, will lead to the creation of a 'theme-park Berlin' is a cause of constant tension. Because artists can afford to live and work, the work itself doesn't seem as bent to the whims of commercial or pre-established art world vehicles or as susceptible to co-option by local commercial forces. The mythology of Berlin and the artists' 'based-in-Berlin' identity keeps the scene alive, but the sales take place largely outside of Berlin.

It seems fitting to hypothesise that a city so full of layered influences should breed a hybrid outlook evident in, for example, the work of Kreuzberg-born artist Timur Si Qin or the recent exhibition *The Still-Life of Vernacular Agents* at Kraupta-Tuskany Gallery. The conflation of imagery in the work of artists like Timur and Oliver Laric is, much like the city itself, a palimpsest.

Berlin can seem the mistress to London's wife: a transient city through which people pass looking for escape or redemption, before they return to routine. But there are signs that this might be changing. The arrival of Soho House, combined with the launch of *Frieze de* (based out of Berlin) suggests that it might be increasingly simplistic to understand Berlin as innocent utopia. Oliver Laric said, when I asked him what was good about Berlin, 'no hierarchy'. It remains to be seen whether this can hold true, but artist Cecile B. Evans points out that this might have positive ramifications for artists in the city: 'the 'based-in-Berlin' tag has become a commitment to this scene and period. For a while, before I arrived [in 2009] it seemed that everyone was between Berlin and somewhere else – based in London and Berlin, based in New York and Berlin – as though one needed a larger, more established city. That is changing'. People have been saying that Berlin is dead for years.

Berlin creates its own reality. Ideas more easily become actions here. One can survive on speech acts and declaratives: 'I am a...' and get away with it, for a time at least. Is Berlin a myth? Perhaps. But myths become legends and form narratives which structure and buttress our reality, a future willed into existence through imagination. Berlin is a self-fulfilling prophecy.

Creative Stasis in
a Post-Industrial Utopia
Daniel Udy

The colonisation of urban enclaves by creative communities has punctuated art history from Dada-era Paris to 1960s New York. Writing in *Frieze* ('Changing Places', Summer 2012), sociologist Sharon Zukin described us as 'canaries in the mine of gentrification', perpetually carving out new territories in which to live and work before the inevitable arrival of developers hoping to capitalise on our presence. This process has been widely theorised, and will be familiar to anyone who has witnessed the rise and fall of neighbourhoods touted as 'bohemian' or 'creative': artists are drawn by cheap rents and plentiful space to a dilapidated or marginalised area; this injection of cultural capital attracts the left-leaning branch of the middle classes; gentrification takes hold and is followed by regeneration through publicly-funded galleries, museums and public arts projects. The story ends with increased rents forcing the artist migrants out in search of somewhere new: we are agents of our own displacement, and very much implicated in that which we bemoan.

The inhabitation of urban and industrial areas is a geographical manifestation of the avant garde ideology, with the migration of artists to marginalised neighbourhoods reflecting an antipathy towards wider society. The cyclical process of colonisation, gentrification and relocation mimics the endless game of cat-and-mouse between the avant garde and mainstream culture, and appeals to those self-consciously operating on the fringes of convention. Zukin takes the example of New York's SoHo district and the evolution of 'Loft Living' as a desirable lifestyle aesthetic after the colonisation of former industrial spaces by artists in the sixties and seventies, a development that has exerted huge influence upon subsequent generations (*Loft Living: Culture and Capital in Urban Change*). The notion of artistic community is tied to these localities of time, geography and architecture. But our own era, however we define it, is characterised by uncertainty. Postmodernism heralded the end of the avant garde / mainstream binary, and SoHo's conversion can be viewed as its dying breath in terms of fringe communities.

So what role has Berlin had to play in this navigation of our cultural landscape? The stories of SoHo are passed down from our artistic forebears through retrospectives and art school curricula, formulating the mythos of an avant garde climate defined as much by the industrial landscape in which it operated as the works which were produced. We share a peculiar nostalgia for a time we never experienced in which artistic production was seemingly more radical, born from a sense of community no longer possible in the era of globalisation. Whether such historical schemata are accurate is beside the point: there exists an idealistic longing for such a place, and the fall of the Soviet Union opened East Berlin to fill this void. The division and reunification of the city led to a warped variation of the artist district model, and it is the particularities of the clash between East and West German architecture which make Berlin so unique.

The post-Wall exodus from East to West enabled a wave of young artists to take advantage of cheap rents and the multitude of empty spaces left behind, and while its socio-geographical development is covered in greater detail elsewhere in this publication, it is important to note that the plethora of industrial space was and is not limited to one distinct neighbourhood. Instead, the post-Soviet variant of a 'Loft Living' aesthetic spreads across half of reunified Berlin, and the renovation of vacant buildings into multi-purpose venues such as clubs, galleries and restaurants contributes to this sense of renewal: many young artist migrants are barely older than the reunified city itself, and as such we feel drawn by the possibility of helping to shape its development.

Even considering recent rises in rent and living costs, working in Berlin is much cheaper for British artists than London. The stream of migrants refuses to diminish, with the newest arrivals simply moving to areas further east than those occupied by their predecessors. Numbers continue to rise, stories spread back home and the mythos grows of a place where rents are low, studio space is plentiful and every second person is an artist too.

The effect of this continued migration is a demographic akin to the art schools from which many new arrivals have recently departed. Art school stimulates creative activity through the sharing of ideas, while the pressures of a learning-orientated environment necessitate production. In Berlin, however, the sprawling artistic community is characterised by an absence of pressure. The mythos of a post-industrial creative utopia seems to hold true for newcomers, but it comes at the cost of the productivity and social diversity that invigorates artistic production. Without the educational and financial pressures it is possible to exist as an artist without producing art, and the danger is of stagnation.

Berlin has fostered a space for creative expression, and much exciting new work has emerged from the city. Its reputation has, however, been its undoing. The lack of existential pressure, and the increasingly homogeneous expat community has led to a creative stasis. Berlin continues to appeal to those longing for a post-industrial artist's enclave, but whether inspiration comes as part of the package is another question altogether.

Creative Stasis in a Post-Industrial Utopia

Ohne dem Haus

Robert Rapoport

74–80

The Schimmelfenghaus was situated at the northern end of Breitscheidplatz, between the jagged steeple of the Gedächtniskirche and Bahnhof Zoo. The film *Ohne dem Haus* was shot on its top floor in the two weeks before it was demolished to make way for the tallest building in Berlin.

In its final days the building provided a kind of liminal space. It was an obstacle to what the city was always becoming. I wrote a script about the building's final inhabitant – a bankrupt architect, Ralf, who turned his office into his home, refusing to sign it over to developers. Ralf frames and is framed by this threshold and thus takes on something of the stylite – elevated by his withdrawal. As any good stylite finds, the world won't leave them alone.

The strange asceticism that the Wall granted Berlin explains some of its appeal today. And yet every additional pilgrim dissolves this exceptionalism a bit more. But what do we come for? The sense that one can – like the city itself – arrive by standing still.

CAST

Hannes Hellmann – *Ralf (HR)*; Rainer Strecker – *Leo*; Maike Möller – *Maren*; Bernd Grawert – *Chucky Steinhaus*; Elisabeth Hofmann – *Bes*

CREW

Robert Rapoport – *Regisseur*; Maurice Wilkerling – *Kameramann*; Jonas Römmig – *Oberbeleuchter*; Konstantin Wolkenstein – *Second Unit Kamera*; Isabella Poosch – *Produktion*; Peter Hofknecht – *Filmtonmeister*; Georg Petzold – *Cutter*

Ohne dem Haus

Ohne dem Haus

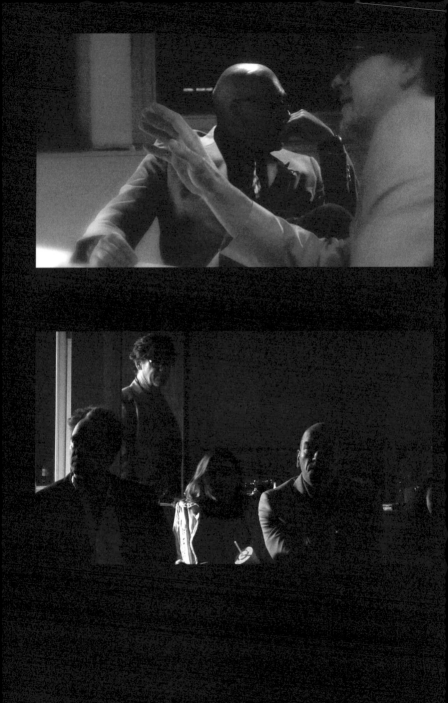

Ohne dem Haus

The Impossible Desire for a Possible Centre / The Possible Desire for an Impossible Centre

Donatien Grau

It is quite difficult to challenge the idea that human life finds its roots in, and is based on, the irrepressible dream of finding a centre. This centre could be defined in personal terms – life, love, children, company, care – or in social terms – achievements, success. Maybe centres exist around us, and outside of us, but our main goal is to enter the spheres they represent, and, as much as we can, become part of them. We constantly experience a desire for possible centres.

The very tragedy of life may well be that this desire often proves to be quite impossible to fulfill, as we cannot be part of this dream-like centre. Emmanuel Levinas once said that the dynamics behind Proust's *À la recherche du temps perdu* all come from the fact that it features an 'aristocracy deprived of Versailles'. It is a world that has lost its centre, and this loss enables the novelist to find another centre, that stands outside of the world in which he lives. And he names it 'literature'.

By so doing, Proust brings to the visible world the paradigm of most human beings' existence: since possible centres prove to be an impossible desire, the desire for an impossible centre becomes possible. Or to put in less cryptic words, we become passionate about centres we know are impossible, and, while being aware of the fact that their very nature is impossibility, we seize them – 'literature', 'art', 'eternal life through literary or artistic glory' to name a few. However, even if we are deeply aware of how unlikely it is for this impossible centre to last, we still tend to believe in it, and, as we believe in it, we sometimes succeed in making it happen in the actual world – or it happens in its own movement… That is the paradox of faith. As a consequence of the strength of a possible desire, an impossible centre becomes reality.

The Impossible Desire…

All those comments might seem, again, rather cryptic and even problematically so. Nonetheless, it is quite clear that this general human schema is exactly the rule governing the reality of Berlin as a centre. Berlin is a centre that is a non-centre. It is the centre of non-centres. In that sense, as an 'outsider amongst centres', the city has been given the possibility to play both parts, so to speak – to be presented simultaneously as a centre and a non-centre.

Until the Reunification, the city had never really been a centre, neither from a political point of view nor from an artistic perspective. From a political point of view, until 1701, it was simply the capital of the Duchy of Brandenburg, that the Elector Frederick turned into the Kingdom of Prussia. Even after the intense architectural projects launched by the kings of Prussia, notably Frederick the Great, the city remained very much provincial. And when it became a centre, it was only one centre amongst centres. This situation remained the same after Berlin became the capital of the German Empire, which was nothing but a recreation of the Holy Roman Empire, under Prussian leadership, but not under the King and Emperor's hegemony.

Regional states kept a considerable part of their authority and Berlin, although the nearest thing to a centre, was a city amongst other cities in Germany. In artistic terms, the situation was very much the same: when the legendary art historian Hugo von Tschudi was fired by the Emperor Wilhelm from his position as Director of the Nationalgalerie, he left to head the Neue Pinakothek in Munich, which he directed until his death.

Other cities were alternatives to the capital. In creative terms, we should not forget that Die Brücke was founded in Dresden, and Der Blaue Reiter in Munich – Bavaria then appeared to be the main centre for the arts in Germany.

Certainly, in the time of National Socialism, the leaders of the regime aspired to make it an actual capital – which it had never been. But they did not succeed. Albert Speer's plans for a 'Germania' were left as unaccomplished projects. In artistic terms, life under the Third Reich was not extremely favourable to avant-gardes. After the war ended, and as the country and the city were divided, Berlin was quite evidently in no condition to be a centre: if galleries such as René Block and Michael Werner first opened there, they either closed or left for another city. Berlin-based artists such as A. R. Penck or Georg Baselitz, moved away and settled in the actual centres of German art – Düsseldorf and then Cologne. If anyone had then asked what the centre of the German art world was, the answer would have certainly been those two cities, from creative, institutional, and financial points of view.

Even today, there is not one single centre in the German art world – the Städelschule in Frankfurt remains a strong place for the arts, as does Cologne as a whole. It is quite obvious that Berlin has taken a growing part within the last decade, but this part is to be put into perspective in the German context itself. Indeed, when foreign artists and creative minds started to arrive in Berlin, in the late 1990s, the city was on the verge of becoming an organised political centre, but was little more than the ruins of the centre it once could have been. As a centre, it was a total outsider – no one would have expected it to hold such a position.

Its exploded geography, its lack of contemporary cultural institutions, its lack of money – as the Mayor Klaus Wowereit phrased it: 'arm aber sexy'. At that time, the city was certainly

The Impossible Desire…

poor, and not really sexy. But in the same way as Cicero once said 'summus ius, summa iniuria' – 'the more justice, the more injustice' – the least 'sexy' was probably 'sexy' in its own right. In that sense, its achievement in progressively becoming one appears to be the exact illustration of the principle we enunciated earlier: entering a possible centre is an impossible desire – almost unachievable, because the possible centre does not have the structure to remain so. However, reaching an impossible centre certainly appears as a likeable, therefore possible goal. Berlin was, in many respects, an impossible centre – both inside and outside of Germany. Inside of Germany, it was part of a tradition in which there was no unique centre for the arts – a situation comparable to the case in Italy.

Outside of Germany, the 'Berlin moment' happened at a time when centrality seemed no longer to be the issue. In the literary field, the emergence of writers such as Salman Rushdie, Mario Vargas Llosa, Gabriel García Márquez, Wole Soyinka, proved that masterpieces were not longer the privilege of the Western European and Northern American traditions. Cultural centres existed outside of this limited universe, and they were keen on seizing from them the relevance of the past and taking it elsewhere. In that sense, the 1960s, 1970s and 1980s were a moment of considerable cultural change,experienced by the literary world before the art world. Of course, from the 1990s onwards, the arts became openly polycentric.

Then, the international and national contexts can be compared in the early 2000s, Germany's many centres needed a new political, artistic and cultural unity. At the same time, the art world's many centres, then aware of their relevance, needed a centre. Polycentrism needed monocentrism in order to remain relevant. Nonetheless, this new centre could not be a traditional one. It was not a traditional cultural centre, such as Paris, New York, or London. Neither was it an emerging commercial megalopolis, such as Hong Kong, Shanghai. It had to exist in a totally different context, within a dialogue between absolute openness to the future and intense relation to the past. And that was Berlin. It bore so much history and at the same time appeared, after the reunification, as the 'terra nova', if not totally 'incognita'. Berlin was the twin of what Vienna had once been: the centre of Europe, and, in a way, the centre of Western creation at the beginning of the 20th century. The capital of the Austrian-Hungarian Empire existed in a twofold situation: extremely local, even provincial, and unbelievably global. Berlin had both aspects in its DNA. This coexistence made it a difficult place to stabilise and to keep growing culturally, artistically and intellectually. Indeed such difficulty was a main reason why the city appeared to be so exciting. Everything was possible and impossible at the same time, and both identities were brought together by the most recent events – both from a purely German point of view, and from an international perspective. Berlin was the place people believed in to be the impossible centre. And that possible belief made it happen – made the impossible become a reality.

Berlin Heute

John Holten

88–90

Berlin today? What to say – today like every day in Berlin you're either making a memory or remembering one. It's summertime right now so it feels like the days are full of potential, and Neukölln's street corners are full of difficult love affairs and cheap food. It's a tumultuous place. Things are changing. Sometimes you worry that Berlin is changing too much – gentrification debates aside – that the rules are getting stricter, that you won't be able to drink a beer on the U-Bahn, or have a barbecue anywhere other than on seven designated park corners, because Berlin today is all about these little freedoms you don't get elsewhere. It's a state of mind, of relaxed indifference. To put it another way: Berlin is the best place to fall in love because of the easiness towards life it breeds in its denizens. But then again, it might also be the most difficult place to fall in love for the same reason.

Berlin has its seasons and they determine what today can mean. It's hard to write about Berlin today because I know it will be different tomorrow. I got a contract phone today, having always paid as I went. Four years here and still acting as if I'm passing through, but today I put down another root. After that I walked up Neukölln's plateau (which now hosts the world's most unique urban park, formerly Tempelhof airport) to my office, where I sat all afternoon looking out of the storefront windows at the hip and old, Berliner's fresh or ancient, clients to the two brothels across the street, the unemployed, immigrants, the rich, the leisure class. I do some proofreading, I check upcoming events. I edit a press release for a show by The LGB Group in Milan. I promote an exhibition opening tonight in New York in which The LGB Group are discussed. In Berlin today, I'll go now for a drink on Weserstraße, Neukölln's café and bar

Berlin Heute

strip, to meet someone who works for another online art blog. After that I'll participate in something called Philosophical Football that involves red wine, joints and nonsense. Today I predict with confidence I'll bump into at least one friend on my way home and we'll stop a while and chat, perhaps sit a moment and watch the city pass by. It's July right now, so in many ways today will be endless.

You can do things in this city; you can also do nothing. There's something in this that makes Berlin a good place to make art. Berlin is not a lazy place, it has its public debt and shrinking labour market but the city today is a monument to industriousness: and determination. As the seat of the German government Berlin is synonymous with rigorous economic control, the best pupil in class. Government fiscal policy hasn't anything much to do with living and creating art, but it shouldn't be forgotten, this ability to get things done, to fix what has been broken, unite apparent opposites.

Today it remains possible to make art in Berlin. Studios can still be acquired cheaply enough in Wedding or Neukölln, and there are plenty of small spaces to show new work. There are commercial spaces to cart your portfolio around to, and there are the openings and the bars and clubs. Bar Drei or La Chat Gris for the Mitte crowd, O Tannenbaum for the Neukölln crowd, the PORK night at Ficken3000 for the gay crowd, Times for the American, Berlin-as-New York's-sixth-borough-crowd, the list could go on. Or, this being Berlin, change.

Berlin, being a city full of people coming from elsewhere, has scenes that are perhaps less initially daunting or closed as in more static places. The air, like the trains coming and going to Paris or Warsaw, flushes things out, keeps it feeling fresh. You can create your own scene, your own crowd. You rarely feel lonely for long.

Is Berlin fresh today? There are lots of tired-out, bitchy expats to be found; but they'll leave soon enough. Berlin is about missing it when you're not here, and making plans to leave when you are. One of the peculiarities of the Berlin art scene is still that, to make a living of it, it needs to be shown elsewhere. Artists in Berlin still have to apply for shows and residencies beyond the city. While Berlin's art market can't compare with London or New York for prices realised, there is a culture of friends buying art at cheap prices, swapping work or founding small businesses. There are legion examples: the artist duo Mariana Caló and Francisco Queimadela are part of the team that run Altes Finanzamt, the artists Sol Colero and Christopher Kline run the gallery Kinderhook and Caracas and the press Feather Troat. Javier Peres is art dealer, gallerist, artist. Artists open bars, play in bands, DJ. Berlin encourages this type of crossover.

Berlin today is a testing ground, a sounding board. It is a place to share with peers. In this respect it has an effect comparable to altermodern rain, a precipitation that comes to ground not in Berlin, but beyond, when these encounters and enterprises are taken on journeys, exported, leave town for a while.

Colour Plates

92

Viktor Timofeev
Cloudcatcher (2012)
Ink on inkjet print
7 × 12 cm

93

Julia Prezewowsky
Declarations – Monument for Nonsense (2008 – 2012)
Sculpture, performance and installation

94

Viktor Timofeev
Cloudsync (2012)
Coloured pencil, graphite on inkjet print
20 × 30 cm

95

Jan Kaesbach
Berlin Calling (2011)
Telephone and plinth

96

Nick Jeffrey
Black (2008 – 2009)
Oil and emergency blanket on linen
145 × 135 cm

97

Jan Kaesbach
Picture for Jeff (2012) Installation shot
Gyclée print, shelf, light box, loupe, 8 slides

98

Jennifer Mustapha & Erin Hughes
Berlin Intervention (2012) Installation shot

Berlin's Art Market: Between Ambition and Reality

Fact Sheet

100 – 102

Artist income[1]

- Buyers in Berlin galleries are Berlin clients
- Other German nationals
- International clients

Berlin's Art Market: Between Ambition and Reality

Berlin's art scene is buzzing. Freelance artists and cultural aficionados from all over the world flock to the city like the faithful to temple. Word gets around quickly: Berlin is a bohemian paradise, offering five-room Soviet style apartments in centrally located *plattenbau* high rises for very little money; dingy bars / clubs / exhibition spaces pop up in occupied basements, and weekly gallery opening marathons tempt spectators with free rounds of Aperol Spritz.

The promotion of the Berlin lifestyle is supported by the race for superlatives in news articles about the art scene, circulated by the city and its representatives of the creative industry: the German art market is generating the third largest revenue in all of Europe. In 2002, it rendered *c.* 800 million euros. Of all European cities, Berlin hosts the largest amount of galleries: an estimated amount of 650 galleries in 2009. Of all German cities, Berlin has the highest density of self-employed artists. In 2005, *c.* 20,000 artists lived and worked in Berlin, an increase of 40% since the millennium.[1]

It is fun for those who come to get their quick fix of the scene before moving on to other things, but what about all the complaints from those who came to stay?

The largest artist association in Berlin, the bbk e.V., and smaller individual artists' collectives have voiced their concerns about increasing rent prices and lack of funding and support from the local government. It doesn't take much research to find out that the Fine Arts are clearly not a priority of Berlin's cultural politics. Looking at the city's entire cultural budget spent in 2010 (*c.* 420 million euros), one can see that the Fine Arts only received only four million, which equals only 1% of the entire cultural budget volume, and that tiny portion is continuously diminished by spending cuts.[2]

Perhaps the reason for this can be found when looking at the numbers in a bigger context, which reveal that a vital art scene and the sheer quantity of art, producers and distributors, do not necessarily translate into big money. After all, Germany's art market share, third largest in Europe it may be, is only at a meagre 2.7 % in a global comparison. Among the different branches of the creative sector based in Berlin, the art market has a comparatively high amount of businesses in operation; however, they also happen to generate the least income. A study predicts that the revenue per gallery will be 50% less in Berlin than the national average.

All of these findings suggest that in economic terms, Berlin's art market is negligible compared to that of other locations, nationally and internationally. This means that while people come to Berlin to look at art and to experience the lifestyle and atmosphere that surround it, they are simply not willing to pay for it.

That is the blessing and the curse of a city that still promises that the best things in life are free.

Written and researched by Henrike Dessaules

1   Fine Arts Berlin, 2009, fineartsberlin.com
2   bbk berlin e.V., March 2011

Aelyn Belyn
Katie Paterson

In November 2010, I initiated a temporary residency project in Berlin with sixteen students and staff from Edinburgh College of Art's Drawing and Painting Department, and we presented our work at Matthew Bown Gallerie: *Aelyn Belyn*.

Aelyn Belyn emerged between us from a shared desire to set up a residency-situation which could enable a variety of site-related projects; artworks, events, interventions, and happenings, where the emphasis was on place, locality, time, context and space. Berlin was chosen as our destination, for its complex layering of historical and contemporary culture, and the richness and diversity of its spaces: green space, urban space, day-life, night-life, from metropolis skylines to barren and uncontrolled landscapes. Berlin allows a level of freedom not readily found elsewhere. Amongst the openness of its citizens and the plethora of artistic, performative, underground and guerrilla activities, we could carry out our fieldwork in an un-self-conscious way.

Our intention was for the project to have no defined limits; we wanted a space where we could experiment, be inventive and open in our responses to the city. An exhibition was planned, not to present finished artworks, but as a situation to bring together ideas, proposals, exchanges.

A great deal of preparation followed – talks, proposals, workshops, meetings and cake-and-bakes, and our blog (aelynbelyn.blogspot.de) became an essential way for us to share information and ideas. Projects were thought through in advance, to then become undone and reformed during our journeys.

I don't believe any of us could have foreseen the colossal energy and drive, the spontaneity and creativity, connections and friendships that were to evolve during the residency.

Aelyn Belyn

Living and working communally promoted a collective spirit and closeness, where conversations were open, working methods shared and where natural collaborations arose.

H France, still from *Left Eye / Right Eye*. Five minute looped DVD. Developed within the context of the *Aelyn Belyn* project.

Each day, individually and as a group, we explored sites from colour towers and observatories, to dance halls, forests, runways, abandoned funfairs and listening stations. We unraveled the city and its energy merged with ours. We explored Berlin with a psychogeographic approach; it encouraged wanderings, journeys, meanderings and delvings. Artwork formed through this direct experience of the city, and the shift of awareness and heightened responsiveness created through being in unfamiliar territories.

We shared ideas and findings in meetings, and our work merged with our research. Amongst many other things, we found ourselves dancing in Devil's Mountain, listening to derelict railway lines, watching a galaxy lift off, transmitting our thoughts through space, inverting walls, charting trees, growing architecture, freezing wasps and filming the sky in three-dimensions. As our artwork was brought together at Matthew Bown Gallerie, a common thread emerged as that of translation, passage and displacement between people, thoughts, forms, objects and things.

R Barron, R King & M De Laborde still from *Ballroom Dancing at Teifelsberg.* Three minute looped DVD. Developed within the context of the *Aelyn Belyn* project.

Aelyn Belyn provided us with a crucial interruption, a situation outside of the studio and our familiar surroundings which opened up new and unexplored approaches and challenged our everyday ways of working. The memories and experiences are a continuing influence.

ARTISTS

Jessica Argo, Rachel Barron, Rachael Cloughton, Claire Adams Ferguson, Karen Forbes, Hazel France, Rachel King, Hannah Knights, Manuela De Laborde, Faith Limbrick, Claire MacCrory, Katie Paterson, Grace Sherrington, Peter Skibinski

Aelyn Belyn

Hello to Berlin

Vid Simoniti

I arrived in Berlin on an oppressively grey, dead day of winter.
I was to stay with my friend in Köpi – I didn't realise it then,
but living in the legendary squat on Köpenicker Straße was
something of a badge of honour among the city's underground scene. Back then I was pretty clueless. I rocked up
in an aggressively normal winter coat from Zara and a borr-
owed suitcase on wheels. A punk defleaing her dog shot me
a murderous look. 'Wohnt hier Peter D...? Ein Engländer...'
I asked timidly. 'Yes', she said in English with a heavy Spanish
accent. 'Up. Second floor.'

People like myself, Pete and the Spanish girl were part
of the budget airline generation. We wouldn't have liked the
name, but we were easyjetters. In our twenties we poured into
Berlin from all parts of Europe, myth-chasers on orange and
yellow-blue birds. The trail blazed by previous generations of
adventurous Western expats, who saw in the squatter culture
of West Berlin an oasis of the radical left, was now a royal
road paved by the common currency, pre-crisis prosperity
and cheap flights. Casual workers, students, anarchists,
layabouts, romantics, gap years, Erasmus students, Americans
on the grand tour, and of course artists. We all flocked in.
No one I knew had a job or very clear aspirations. People
came for the city itself and what it represented; Berlin was
a byword among Europe's twenty-somethings for an alternative, bohemian existence. There was something mythical
about the place.

A myth, likely, is not just a particular atmosphere that
hangs around the city like graffiti. It's a story. And though
Berlin does not have a founding myth, like Rome, the popular

myth associated with it today is one of continuous death and rebirth, of destruction and liberty. That's not the same as the myth of a decadent golden age; Berlin is not like Imperial Rome or the Paris of the Belle Époque or the New York of Mary Boone. These were all cities that indulged in excess when most convinced of their power and prosperity. The myth of Berlin is different: the period of bohemia and artistic activity comes right after a fall. It is not unlike the myth of Hyacinthus or Adonis, the myth of a felled youth whose blood nourishes a fantastic floral growth. An image that has stuck with me from my first visit: Peter and I climbed an abandoned factory on the Spree and found birch trees, sprouting out of the roof's sheer concrete.

Berlin is full of such memorials to toppled hubris. The twelve metre tall soldier at the head of the gargantuan Soviet War Memorial in Treptower Park is no longer visited by solemn parades, but rather by young revellers skinny-dipping in the nearby lake or partying on the Insel der Jugend. Teufelsberg, an abandoned US spying station in the Western part of the city, is now popular for its impromptu concerts, and its nudist beach on the adjoining lake. The notorious Berghain nightclub, located in a former electricity plant, is perhaps the prime symbol of the German cult of industry converted into a temple to Dionysian self-effacement.

Stern-faced goliaths of bygone regimes lie obsolete, broken and unstirring, and Berlin's insouciant flora and fauna sprout out of every crack and orifice.

2

The myth is made by those who tell it, and Berlin has hosted a veritable army of storytellers. Four, in particular, have come to epitomise the times in which they lived: Alfred Döblin, Christopher Isherwood, Christiane F and Thomas Brussig.

Döblin and Isherwood document the two sides of Weimar Berlin. Döblin's 1929 masterpiece *Alexanderplatz Berlin*, which immerses the reader in a world of petty crime around the famous square, is a hallmark of German modernism made popular by a cult TV series directed by Rainer Werner Fassbinder. Isherwood's works *Mr Norris Changes Trains* (1935) and *Goodbye to Berlin* (1939) present a more light-hearted portrayal of Berlin's bohemian circles, and would also gain greater fame through their adaptation for film, as the musical *Cabaret*.

Christiane F and Brussig are the defining myth-makers of post-war Germany. Christiane F's *Wir Kinder vom Bahnhof Zoo* (1979) is a first person account of a 14 year-old heroin addict and prostitute, showcasing the dark reality bubbling underneath the libertine spirit of West Berlin. Kids from the Gropiusstadt tower blocks shoot heroin and listen to David Bowie. Brussig's *Helden wie wir* (1995) is written from an East German's perspective, recounting the fall of the Wall in less melodramatic terms than the *Lonely Planet* (apparently, we all have the protagonist's penis to thank). These four writers have each helped to provide Berlin with one of the several aspects of the myth of Berlin: they have given us a Berlin to imagine, to believe in.

Berlin has crumbled into dust three times, then, and three times a myth has grown on the ruins. But as palpably as its latest instantiation may be felt on the ground, the mythical bohemian Berlin that has been in development since the mid 1990s has not yet been solidified into a recognisable artistic vision. There have been a few attempts here and there (notably in the work of young local filmmakers such as Hannes Stöhr), but nobody has yet been able to articlate with the lucidity of the authors I've mentioned: no one has yet to grasp the strange mixture of radical politics, oppositional lifestyle and artistic prowess that currently throbs in the city. Brussig's more recent book, *Berliner Orgie*, is set in the Berlin of today but puts forward a much more unsentimental, much more local, much more German understanding of the city than that which informs Berlin's art production. The myth that so many unsteady dwellers of Kreuzberg and Neukölln have come to inhabit over the last two decades has, arguably, not yet been given a definite form.

A lot hangs on that. Whether or not the Berlin of the early twenty-first century will enter posterity as a mythical place depends, in part, on whether a specific account emerges to define the future's understanding of the city. Artists are the keepers of our shared notions of what a particular place is or was; think of Dickens' London, Proust's Paris, Durrell's Alexandria or Tom Wolfe's New York. It seems possible that the visual arts rather than literature will fulfil this function, as they have done in the past. Toulouse-Lautrec, Otto Dix, Picasso and Warhol, to name a few, have done much to define our contemporary interpretation of their times and cities. It's too soon to say who will do this for Berlin.

3

It might be that more time must pass for the contemporary myth of Berlin to find expression. But it might be, too, that post-reunification Berlin has not merited a mythical portrayal. It might be that a certain lack of vision, a lack of artistic unity, is in fact a defining characteristic of the political and artistic movements that have flourished after the fall of the Wall, and that this decadence for its own sake does not lend itself to the establishment of a coherent myth.

Each generation to come after Paris 1968 and Woodstock 1969 has been accused of conformism by its predecessor. Berlin is no different: every expat despises those who came after her and bemoans the city's gentrification since the early 1990s. Whatever critical edge Berlin is perceived to have had, many now think it lost. The mantra is familiar: the commercial Gallery Weekend has replaced artists' squats; yummy mummies have stormed Prenzlauer Berg; Berghain has become a tourist attraction; boys and girls with fake prescription glasses, MacBooks and linen carrier bags have driven the punks out of Kreuzberg. The rough edges have been smoothed away. The myth of Berlin today, we might think, is indeed a *mere myth*: an exaggerated and idealised belief to be disproved.

But there are reasons to dismiss this cynicism. Berlin maintains a genuine political edge, as is visible in the art produced and exhibited in the city. The 2012 Berlin Biennale addressed recent ruptures in the social consensus, and opened itself up to new political movements like Occupy. Whether this has any political effect remains subject to dispute, of course, but there can be no doubt that of the major

European cities, Berlin's art scene remains the most politically engaged. Looking beyond the visual arts to the broader sphere of culture – to the party scene, theatre, music, even to opera or just café conversation – it is clear that Berlin is serious about its politics. The shutting down of nuclear power plants in Germany came as a direct response to the mobilisation of the people – not just in Berlin, of course, but also in Berlin. And that is a considerable feat.

In addition to this, Berlin continues to offer alternatives to the regimented consumerist existence of contemporary Western, urban life. People go out of their way to form meaningful communities. The WG culture of flat sharing, in which more is expected from new inhabitants than that they simply share the rent, feels a world apart from London. I briefly lived in a flat that took communal meals four times a week, and each person had to spend an hour a week teaching other flatmates a useful skill (I picked up knitting). Flats are organised around specific ideologies and identities; a friend applied for a polyamorous community (she didn't get in).

In Berlin it still feels possible to disdain the rat race, to pursue a life free of the narcissism and greed that that seem inescapable elsewhere. This is partly because Berlin is still quite good at resisting normativity, the sense that we must desire to be normal by consuming the normal things. Normativity is harder to resist in other cities; even, say, in the supposedly nonconformist East London. The difference between Chelsea and Shoreditch seems to be, too often, a superficial difference in style – Burberry versus Superdry – while the rigour with which a particular identity is shaped and the intensity with which it is enforced is similar. Berlin has less of that. While it has also developed its own subcultures and styles, the city seems to value, undoubtedly also because of its history of totalitarianisms, individual creativity and resistance to any kind of groupthink.

That is why perhaps, art and music scenes are often mocked as hopelessly idealistic and hopelessly unsaleable. What on the whole fails to occur to such commentators is that the artists of Berlin, the kind who make their performances in Görlitzer Park or display their work in an occupied brewery, aren't in it for the money. Which isn't to perpetuate the unhelpful idea that a good artist is a starving artist, but to acknowledge that there is a genuinely different ethos behind art production in Berlin. Indeed, the artists of Berlin are no longer as poor as the myth would have them be, but Berlin art is still best fitted to public spaces, occupied spaces, common spaces. Art is presented as a form of life, rather than a saleable object. And this makes you wonder whether Berlin or London bears the greater curse.

We must acknowledge that Berlin is no longer a city of squatted ruins. One could hardly expect that to remain the case following its reinstatement as the nation's capital. However, Berlin continues to offer an alternative vision of life and of art. We easyjetters spend too much time arguing about the real Berlin, about who got there first, about gentrification, about whether we should be shooting heroin or eating cupcakes. It makes more sense to keep one's ear to the ground and pay attention to what is coming out of the city. Europe is enduring its most troubled period since the Wall come down, and the myth of Berlin now is likely to be defined by the coming ten years. It might be that the past two decades come to be seen yet again as a period of irresponsible bohemianism preceding a fall. Or, as giants continue to crumble all around the continent, Berlin might turn out to be the city that offers a workable alternative to a failed status quo.Its challengers might well turn to Berlin to find lifestyles and artforms to suit a post-capitalist world. This time, it's not goodbye to Berlin just yet.

Interview with Nick Jeffrey
Christina Danick

CHRISTINA DANICK

Why leave London for Berlin?

NICK JEFFREY

I had to leave London. I want really to live somewhere with a great climate, but I've always found that cities are somewhere between where you really want to be.

CHRISTINA DANICK

Did you have any expectations before coming here?

NICK JEFFREY

Not really, I'm still finding my feet. I have friends who work here and I relate to their work quite a bit. We're not like a group of artists, it's quite loose. There are crossovers and influences, which I find really important. But it seems artists are already starting to leave Berlin.

CHRISTINA DANICK

Where are they going?

NICK JEFFREY

Some to Cologne, some back to London. I think the guys I know didn't like the changes that were happening in Berlin.

CHRISTINA DANICK

What are the differences between London and Berlin in regards to living as an artist?

Interview with Nick Jeffrey

It's a lot tougher to live in London, though there is also a very good community. It's always important to have these people to support each other. If you prefer to have a life that's a bit more at peace than I think Berlin is better. It's just a lot calmer. In terms of the art scene, London feels more academic, more serious. You have to have a very serious face on when you work there. Saying that, I don't think there is much difference in the galleries here. Maybe with the younger ones, where everything is a bit more free.

CHRISTINA DANICK

Why do you think big art spaces in London are so successful and similar spaces in Berlin aren't?

NICK JEFFREY

Well, Tate Modern is free. The Hamburger Bahnhof costs €14.

CHRISTINA DANICK

Do you remember the first time you got here? What were your thoughts, impressions?

NICK JEFFREY

Things were a lot more open, I mean for an artist. There were these huge warehouse spaces. But with time they got smaller and followed the pattern of London, with partition walls and higher rents. There are still amazing, huge studios here, but they are very expensive.

CHRISTINA DANICK

But still cheaper than in London?

NICK JEFFREY

Yes, but it's different – landlords here seem to charge more for studio space than living space. It seems people who lived here in the eighties are very angry. Prenzlauer Berg used be quite anarchic. I don't necessarily think it should be that now, but it's become very conservative. There's more protest against gentrification here than in London. In London protest is shut down, while in Berlin there are outlets for anger. In London that doesn't happen, but if it happens then it really happens.

CHRISTINA DANICK

You mean like the riots...

NICK JEFFREY

Yes.

CHRISTINA DANICK

Do think that this gentrification is natural, or do you see it as a negative phenomenon?

NICK JEFFREY

Both. It always happens. Prenzlauer Berg used to be an artists' district like East London, and like that area it's changed. I think South London is the last really artistic area in London. But everywhere changes, and it's natural.

CHRISTINA DANICK

Does working in Berlin change they way you work, or the works themselves?

Interview with Nick Jeffrey

Not really. I think it could do, but this is the second time I've lived here so I'm kind of used to it. When you come here for the first time everything is a surprise.

CHRISTINA DANICK

Do you think there is a myth around Berlin?

NICK JEFFREY

I think it was Tacita Dean who said Berlin is like an island to the rest of Germany. I think that's true. Berlin is always shape-shifting.

Artists' Income
Fact Sheet

Reasons for artists living in Berlin[1]

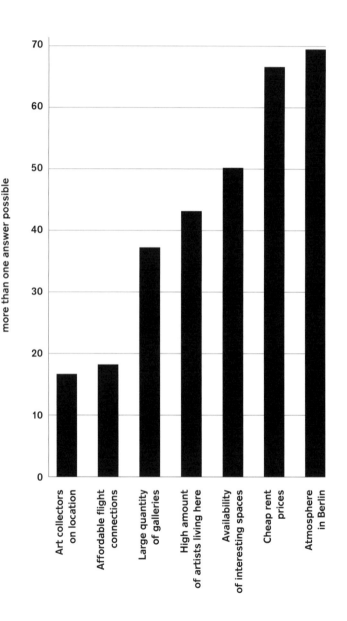

Response in per cent, more than one answer possible

- Art collectors on location
- Affordable flight connections
- Large quantity of galleries
- High amount of artists living here
- Availability of interesting spaces
- Cheap rent prices
- Atmosphere in Berlin

Artist's Income

According to a recent study, the average yearly income of an artist in Berlin is, at 11,612 euros, noticeably below the national average. Only about a fifth of artists can cover their expenses with their art work alone. The majority have to work in unrelated jobs on the side, receive financial support from family and friends or depend on social benefits and Hartz IV (the German version of unemployment benefits). When comparing the art-related income rates of men and women, it becomes obvious that female artists live far more precarious lifestyles than their male colleagues.[1]

A reason for the difficulty in generating income may be that only a tiny fraction of artists are permanently represented by a gallery. The rest have to find other means of promoting their work and getting exhibition opportunities. Freelance artists have claimed to spend up to two thirds of their time with activities related to marketing, acquiring sponsors and applying for funding. Artists have to become self-promoters alongside their artistic practice.

Even gallery representation does not equal immediate financial remuneration. Many artists put more money into getting exhibited than they get out of it, all for the sake of exposure which may or may not lead to eventual fame.

Some artists have now begun to protest these circumstances. They demand a basic income in order to pursue their craft without the existential fears. However, whether these demands will be successful may be even less certain than their success in becoming famous.

Written and researched by Henrike Dessaules

---

1   *Studio Berlin II*, Institut für Strategieentwicklung, June 2011.

Ghost of a Better Future
Samara Grace Chadwick

128 – 132

Other cities are often mere ghosts of a better past; in the hollows of Berlin is possibly – there is no other choice – the ghost of a better future.
– Ernst Bloch

Anyone who has been here knows: there are countless places in Berlin that feel unreal, unhinged. As if floating, unanchored, between various and conflicting meanings. These are places where we newcomers but also true Berliners often get lost. There is elation in these places, in these voids, an unsettling rush of utter disorientation in which the self is suspended in possibility.

Walter Benjamin, a Berliner himself, wrote about the sensation of wandering, lost, in Berlin. He describes a dream of charting an intricate map of his childhood memories: a self-portrait of sorts, drawn across the city's face. For Benjamin, space and identity are inseparable: knowing oneself is an exercise in mapping where one stands.

In these voids, not knowing where we stand, we are unfastened from familiar structures and released into something enticing, unknown. People often call it potential – and, if anything, it is this precise feeling that has drawn so many of us to Berlin. We are artists, thinkers, we are discontent and hopeful. We see Berlin as an open space into which we may pour our true selves, brimming with creativity, unhindered by the nine to five. Berlin will make you happy. Berlin will make you free. Will make you true. Berlin is the sweet antidote to the superfluous clutter of the cities we fled in the name of our creativity, of ideas, of a better future.

Coming to Berlin is thus less an arrival than a departure: from cities like New York, Toronto, London. It is utopian. Utopias have always been political, writes Fredric Jameson, they have always been a critique of the status quo. Indeed, in our articulation of what we are fleeing, we are actively rewriting Berlin as what it is not. Berlin's identity is forged in contrast to the perceived deprivation of previous places.

We come with the assumption that we are new. We remember Berlin when we arrived, *our* Berlin (when rents were half what they are now, before the language in the midday Mitte cafés was a lazy international English, before the city's gritty secrets became hotspots for the neon young: our past selves reflected distastefully back at us) as the *authentic* Berlin.

As though an authentic Berlin ever existed! Rather, it seems Berlin's most persistent quality is its inconsistency. Over ninety years ago, Ernst Bloch moved to Berlin to cure a writer's block he blamed on his native Bavaria. 'I do believe Berlin, the powerful, the utopian, is my city most of all', he writes in an elated entry into his journal. 'In Berlin,' he continues, 'it is especially easy for life to become new. The people have little else behind them to call a place of origin.'

Bloch was a utopian. He believed we needed to engage in creative practices to produce a world in which we are able to realise our deepest dreams. From Berlin, Bloch would begin his great work, *The Principle of Hope,* in which he describes hope as something circular that destroys itself only to be reborn in a new time and a new geography.

Bloch's Hope is the latent charge that fills Berlin's voids. And despite the current push to fill these voids with commerce and bright commodities, they are still everywhere: in the spaces, 100m in width, where the Wall once traced a untrodden path through the city's heart; in the ruins of the flattened city; in the blueprint skeleton of Speer's bombastic *Welthauptstadt.*

In the overgrowth of one of these voids, along the would-be North-South axis, hunched in the brambles, stands the only remaining relic of the would-be city of Germania. You only see it if you're looking for it, but then it overwhelms: an enormous cylindrical cement block, hoisted like a hideous beast on a clumsy foot. The Schwerbelastungskörper stands today as a cold negative for a structure that never was, bearing witness at once to great ambition and to the very impossibility of that ambition.

The Körper weighs the exact 12,650 tonnes of architect Albert Speer's envisioned Triumphbogen, a construction so colossal its arch alone could have contained the Arc de Triomphe. Intended as a temporary structure, the concrete cylinder was erected in 1941 to test the resistance of Berlin's notoriously sandy soils. In order for the ground to withstand the massive Monsterbau of Hitler's Germania, the Körper must not sink more than six centimetres.

The Schwerbelastungskörper sank 18 cm by 1944. By 1945 the soils into which it was thrust had become American.

Berlin built on sand:
They were lovely illusions, reaching high
Built on sand.
They had a touch of paradise.
A spell you can't explain.
For in this crazy paradise
You are in love with pain.
– 'Illusions', sung by Marlene Dietrich in A Foreign Affair (1948)

In no other city can one witness history so intolerant of linearity as Berlin, so complicit with its native son, Benjamin, in disputing the notion of progress based on brute mastery over nature, on the naïve attempt to present the past as it was. Benjamin instead proposes a space in which the past is constantly tumbling over itself into the present, in which everything is ephemeral yet connected, and therefore unending. History in Berlin plays out as Bloch too would have described it: the triumph of Time in renegotiating possibility, the inevitable rebirth and eventual fulfilment of all worthy forms of hope.

We all know Berlin's story since Bloch proclaimed it 'the exciting, unreal city'. We all know it as the stomping ground for so many of the past century's wildest ambitions, the site of boisterous enactments of hope. Now, today, its spaces liberated from a century of suspense, its geographies suspended by the thousand cranes of reconstruction, Berlin welcomes a new generation of hopefuls. Here we all are with our lofty ambitions. We've been here for a few years now: how far have we sunk?

Anyone who has been here knows: there are countless people in Berlin that feel unreal, unhinged. We too have come here to plant ourselves in the soils of Berlin and to see whether our dreams are feasible. We too began with upward hopes, faces to the sky. Soon we ended up entrenched in the Berlin dirt, testing, retracing, and defacing our original plans. And so now we stand, clumsily, like the Schwerbelastungskörper, very much transformed: stripped of our original intentions, strange beacons of what might have been.

Bloch once described the feeling in Berlin as *dieses es-wird-doch-nicht-halten*, 'this it-surely-won't-last'. He would then go on to describe this intangibility as an essential element of hope: the latent, the hopeful, the *Noch-nicht-Gewordenen*, the 'not-yet-become'. Which is what we all are during our time in Berlin: not-yets. The city provides little basis for motion, for ascension, because every intention becomes absorbed and then digested, and doesn't bear much weight: it simply sinks.

Berlin is not where permanence is planned. We thought it was bringing us higher, upwards to our goals. In fact, like the Schwerbelastungskörper, which thrust down rather than up, it brought us deeper into ourselves, confirming who we are by means of who we are not. And often distorting the original dream beyond recognition.

I am thinking about this idea of Hope, and what Berlin has come to represent for the new generation, my generation. In the years since we arrived, our collective hopes, the lives that were promised us, have toppled. Now many of us – not so much in Berlin, but elsewhere – are in the streets, protesting in the name of defunct dreams, in the name of all the hope we invested into a future that will not exist.

> *'Here, in the new town, boredom is pregnant with desires, frustrated frenzies, unrealised possibilities. A magnificent life is waiting just around the corner, and far, far away. It is waiting like the cake is waiting when there's butter, milk, flour and sugar. This is the realm of freedom. It is an empty realm. Here, man's magnificent power over nature has left him alone with himself, powerless. It is the boredom of youth without a future.'* – Henri Lèfebvre

The Berlin That I am Looking at

Martina Schmücker

Leaving Berlin
Berlin, November 2002

Eternal cold misery November 2002. It is the first month
in the year that the sun disappears during the day, and now
I will feel like there is no sun until April. The sun doesn't
really disappear of course, we are not that far north, but
I feel like it does – and nobody can tell me that at this time
of year this city is exciting, or that they are having a good time,
or that anything is good here at all. This is the time of constantly
getting colds. Working outside or in a doorway overnight
doesn't help. It is cold, it is dark, I am skint. My body says get
me somewhere warm and give me better food. Day or night,
this is gloom and misery in black and white – drive out of
Berlin for one to two hours in any direction and I promise you
will be back in Technicolor. My decision is final. I need to get
out of here, as soon as possible.

I need to go somewhere this life might make sense –
somewhere busy, somewhere bright, somewhere I can disappear for a while and find a rhythm, find a script in a corner
that works for me.

I have fallen for a guy who does not want me, at least not
now, at least not in public, and I have paranoid visions of everybody around me smirking. I feel humiliated, but this city is
too small for me to hide, there are not enough of us around.
This place feels like a trap. A dark alley I stumbled into, blind
to the cul-de-sac. I feel big-boned and big-bellied, unbefitt-
ing the parade of tiny intelligent waifs and skinny hipsters,
ON the beat and ON the pulse, constantly ON. I feel unable
to walk away, to move on, to find the exit sign. There is no
ON situation for me in this place. There is just a constant flow

of repeated conversations and exchanges of empty words, meaningless kisses, plans that are never realised, a stream of arrangements to meet and drink coffee, and everybody is always late, except me, because I have nothing else to do other than be in attendance. Watching, waiting, as everybody moves ON – quickly, and with purpose I don't understand. I have nothing to do. I am waiting, and I don't know what for. ON. I'm not on, I am off and out. So the only thing to do is to get out, as fast as possible.

Berlin has no rhythm. Berlin has long silent pauses, and then the S-Bahn comes. The lights change, and you disappear across the road. And then the door falls. Shut. Doors are closed here. Most of the time. And if they are open, that does not mean you can come in. That just means you can stand there wanting to come in, possibly for a long time. Until there is a silent pause in the door frame, suddenly, and then... You're too late, again. I'm partly responsible for closed doors and for the waiting, so maybe it is karma that I'm beginning to feel left outside.

November 2002, and I feel like I am in a town frozen in time. Potsdamer Platz is still a construction site. The city isn't even holding its breath – it just looks like somebody pressed the Pause button. Everything has stopped. Is waiting, in attendance. All this space, and nobody there. The big open dark spaces of any S-Bahn station, the empty, deserted backside of Alexanderplatz. A giant theatre set waiting for – who? Which play? Waiting for more architects, artists, web designers, world weary Americans looking for a hideout; more tourists? When all these building sites are ready, when they are transformed into clean new buildings, will the city just fill up with people? Will this be a city, or just continue to be a playground...

A year ago some guy hanged himself on a tree in Grunewald. We have a new mayor. The city has declared itself bankrupt. The clean up should begin, but won't. The Berlin banking scandal isn't even in the headlines. In slow motion the numbers creep up: 1.2 bn, 4... 6... 21 bn... Invisible money is bleeding out of the invisible political structure of this city, and everybody turns and looks to where there once was a sign, pointing WEST. Saying: Transit. Lifeline. Safety catch. It's not there any more. Did anybody notice this?

It is 4 am and I'm going home, crossing Alexanderstraße at Jannowitzbruecke to cut through to somewhere that will get me home faster than the main roads. The crossing is as wide as a football field; there is nobody here now. Not one car. Not one human. The snow crunching under my boots is the only sound, amplified through the arch of the railway bridge.

Spandauer Straße now, and a car stops behind me. I turn around. A man steps out of the car, alone, and walks towards me. He stops, ten metres away. If I would come with him. If he could give me a lift home, or if I would like to come and have a drink with him, now. He doesn't move. He looks very unsure, surprised, as if he stepped out of the car to do something else, and now can't take back what he said, to me, and now...

Nothing about my clothes says that I could be a working girl, and I'm too far from Oranienburger Straße to be confused with the parading wasps working there. It's only him here, and me. I don't feel scared. He looks scared, now. Maybe I should say yes. Just for curiosity, just to see... Nothing surprising ever happens in my Berlin, anyway. I say, 'No, thanks'. He smiles. He says, 'OK, sorry' and gets into his car. I stand and watch him drive away.

The Berlin That I am Looking at

The big wooden door of the hallway opens and I'm for-given, the dark swallows me. I sink and forget the next twelve hours, until it is dark again, until I have to get back to that other hallway. Until next week. Until next month, next year – until there is a letter in the post, saying that I can pack my bags – that they have opened the emergency exit for me, that I passed the TOEFL test, that I can leave now, can get on the boat – that the wait is over. For now.

Turn Around, Look Back
London, October 2011

Wide-eyed and happy, J. and E. are back from Berlin after the summer. They had a great time, the stories are good, there is a slightly bewildered feeling of detachment in their sentences describing the situations they found themselves in. They can't quite put the experience into words. They think they have been to a great place – but now that the memories are blurring, it's not so clear whether this was anything but a weird, exciting holiday. This is a different Berlin and a diff-erent experience from mine. I look back at a city that is ten years younger than the Berlin these two see now. I spent six years in Berlin before leaving for London in 2003. I have been back since then and often I miss it. I have found no reason to go back for good.

Artist turned dealer: HN Semjon set up the permanent installation KioskShopBerlin (top) in 2001. A series of succesful exhibitions by fellow artists encouraged him to develop the space into Semjon Contemporary (bottom), a commercial gallery.

The Berlin That I am Looking at

Berlin. City of Free Space

Katharina Beckmann, Stefanie Gerke and Nele Heinevetter

140 – 147

Living a myth is an arduous privilege. You must keep up appearances while making the most out of it.

Like an artwork, Berlin is charged with symbols. Its mythological character incorporates values such as bohemian lifestyle, excess and creativity. Like an artwork, its value is negotiated elsewhere: in the eyes of the international and local art scene.[1] To those eyes Berlin is still an Eldorado: emerging artists make their name in the numerous young spaces and the established ones find themselves spacious studios and fresh inspiration from a multi-faceted art scene. Young curators experiment and the established ones take up-and-coming artists to galleries outside the city. Berlin's galleries pride themselves on discovering the talents of tomorrow, and the discoveries are monetised in the art world's epicentres. If you earn your Berlin-credibility, the art world seems to be at your fingertips. That's true to some extent, and works for the happy few. Myth and reality do not diverge much in Berlin. Its mythological parameters are closely associated with the notion of freedom: freedom to move, freedom to reinvent yourself, freedom to work without the exaggerated economic pressure imposed by other creative capitals. The mental freedom that attracts people to Berlin derives from the abundance of physical space.

Berlin is a generous microcosm for it offers an abundance of unused space and thus a multitude of possibilities. In the nineteenth century Berlin was an industrial metropolis. The city's political and financial turbulence forced the relocation or bankruptcy of many of its factories in the first half of the twentieth century, though the built residues remain. Bombings during the Second World War contributed to a massive change in the urban layout, both in the use of various areas of the city and in the large number of gaps to be filled. After reunification, therefore, an impressive quantity of cheap living and workspace was at the disposal of anyone who wanted to produce, present or sell contemporary art.

The re-use of wasteland and empty buildings characterises contemporary Berlin culture: since 1996, the Hamburger Bahnhof Museum of Contemporary art resides in a former train station; in 1999, Kunst-Werke Institute for Contemporary Art completed the refurbishment of their facilities in a former margarine factory; in 2004, the Berlinische Galerie moved into a former glass storage. In the historical heart of Berlin a gap left by the demolished Palace of the Republic – the former GDR parliament building and entertainment center – still awaits the construction of the Humboldt Forum, a multi-purpose cultural facility in the guise of the former city palace.

Despite the gentrification of the city, and the associated uproars, Berlin has continued to live up to its mythological reputation. It has been predicted since the mid-1990s that Berlin's art scene would soon fade. But the constant influx of newcomers and the internal renewal of established residents has kept the myth of Berlin alive – and contributed to its realisation. In 2007, over half of the artists participating in documenta 12 and in the Venice Biennial were based in Berlin.[2]

But how do myth and reality balance in 2012?

There is a large variety of network-based scenes and circles to be found in different districts like the posh, saturated Mitte, the alternative Kreuzberg, the traditionally bohemian Schöneberg or the rough Wedding, where different generations demonstrate their respective artistic expressions with works on different topics and in different media. The unique feature of the scene is its mix: Berlin still has an intrinsic generosity that enables coexistence. From its early days, Berlin has been a polycentric city with a heterogeneous population. The city encourages cohabitation rather than marginalisation.

Hamburger Bahnhof, a former railway station which now serves as the Museum für Gegenwart, part of the Nationalgalerie, Berlin. © Oscar Elias / Alamy

This coexistence is by no means static. Triggered by the initial movements towards East Berlin after 1989, the art scene is constantly reinventing itself by migrating, appropriating district after district – led by the avant-garde, followed by the establishment and then some unfortunate laggards. Giti Nourbakhsch pioneered the 'rediscovery' of the West in 2004. In the architecturally eclectic neighbourhood around Potsdamer Straße, established galleries like Esther

Schipper, Isabella Bortolozzi or Martin Klosterfelde and their persecutors like Supportico Lopez or Tanya Leighton reside in beautiful late-nineteenth century spaces while more and more young galleries such as Chert, Kwadrat or Soy Capitàn nestle in the backyards or low-key retail units of Kreuzberg and Neukölln. Meanwhile, the functional Eastern architecture of Mitte has attracted trend-setters such as Kraupa Tuskany gallery, located on the 4 floor of a 1970s office highrise and representing rising digital art stars.

Some successful protagonists treat themselves to spectacular refurbishments: Christian Boros had a monumental air-raid shelter converted for his private collection. Elmgreen and Dragset turned a former pump station into their studiohouse. Johann König restructures the St Agnes church with the help of the architect Arno Brandlhuber into his new gallery. These are some of the more sensational projects. Wasteland in the middle of the city has allowed artists such as Katharina Grosse to build giant studio complexes. But, most of all, Berlin spares spaces for the adventurous, solitary projects like Studio, an experimental project space next to a betting office on the balustrade of the architectural dystopia of Zentrum Kreuzberg, a massive social housing failure at Kottbusser Tor. Kunstverein Artitude e.V. maintains an entire provision bunker close to the once-rough neighbourhood around Görlitzer Park. Art space Reh Kunst has renovated a historical utopian space wonder from the GDR, a telescopic spatial extension hall amidst the notorious yuppie district Prenzlauer Berg.

Not-for-profit initiatives like project spaces, artists' collectives and Kunstvereine play an important role in the Berlin art scene, because its aura relies on its creative potential.

This potential, it is presumed, is unleashed in alternative venues less concerned with marketable or institutional art production: most not-for-profit initiatives focus on the curatorial discourse of their peers by presenting new artistic positions – such as Autocenter in Friedrichshain – or neglected protagonists as seen at Silberkuppe in Kreuzberg – but not all. Salon Populaire in Tiergarten is hosted by curators and critics who offer a platform for the art scene to discuss its own conditions. Remote Essays & Observations in Wedding is run by an artist couple who invite colleagues according to their ability to formally debate set topics such as 'the mistake' or 'the plinth'. LEAP – Lab for Electronic Arts and Performances – encourages its residents to experiment with technological art and to react to the architectural singularity of their huge space in the Berlin Carrée, a shopping mall amidst the tristesse of Alexanderplatz. Schinkel Pavillon e.V. urges international artists to produce sculptures and installations which react either to the octagonal exhibition space of the garden pavilion or its historical legacy. As a means of self-empowerment for the less influential but also a cheap occupation for the multitude of unemployed artists and curators,[3] the alternative scene is – if not financially supported – commonly cherished as one of the major instigators of the artistic discourse. Ironically, behind those projects are committed individuals, investing their energy and capital. And the same can be said about the built city: in the past ten years innovative architectural projects mostly arose due to private commitment. For example, the architects Arno Brandlhuber and Roger Bundschuh who not only designed their recent cutting-edge houses but also financed them. Creative freedom comes at a price.

The city is renowned among its residents for failing to bring the art scene to its full potential – at least not as far as public and political support is concerned. The commercial protagonists have strived for a successful local art fair format. Artists and curators have kept themselves busy discussing the need of a Kunsthalle[4] and public support systems. Both sides urge the senate to support their efforts financially, instead of skimming the results. The art scene claims to shape the cityscape for the better, triggering gentrification and attracting capital to an otherwise bankrupt city.

The fierce resistance to attempts to unify or brand Berlin's artistic community was apparent in reaction to the 2011 group exhibition Based in Berlin, intended as an international showcase for the city's vibrant art scene. The idea of a performance showcase presenting young, Berlin-based artists, in a temporary art gallery to be constructed in the Humboldt Hafen – a development area the city tries to sell to private investors – caused huge controversy. The 'to have and to need' initiative was formed and an open letter signed by artists and curators called for a boycott. The group exhibition was granted €1.6 m[5] – an enormous budget considering the annual €4 m municipal budget for artists, projects and institutions. As a consequence of the clamour, the show was presented in a condemned studio building in Monbijou Park next to the Museum Island as well as in existing institutions such as KW Institute for Contemporary Art, Hamburger Bahnhof, the state-run Berlinische Gallerie and Neuer Berliner Kunstverein n.b.k., and even integrated local art spaces. The curators and their scouts selected 80 artists, only a handful of whom came from the open submissions policy – the majority represented by renowned though relatively young galleries. Although the exhibition was internationally promoted and supported by prominent advisers like Klaus Biesenbach, Christina Macel and Hans Ulrich Obrist. The echo was embarrassingly ambivalent.[6] Berlin understood the challenge of acting out an attributed role.

Berlin's appeal to the art world persists. But as the attention rises, competition increases. Berlin is the base for more than 8,000 artists; over 400 galleries and numerous exhibition venues compete.[7] At the same time opportunities decrease: foreign investor-driven development means affordable spaces are on the decline. Poor districts divest rather than maintain vacant properties, and the temporary re-use of existing structures for cultural purposes has become alarmingly rare. We must hope that the critical voices calling for the heterogeneity of a city shaped by cultural production to be preserved will be heard.[8] The relocation of C/O Berlin gives reason for hope. The private institution was supposed to move from the former Royal Post Office, sold to investors, to the aforementioned studio house in Monbijou Park, which was supposed to be renovated for temporary use instead of being demolished. This solution might now fail because of building law regulations.[9] Just as public interest contributed to preserve the old studio house, so the Kreuzberg population banished the BMW Guggenheim Lab to Prenzlauer Berg – stating they disliked gentrifying art projects.

The city of Berlin sells its potential, and the art scene tries to create a sustainable base for the hype. The successful format of Gallery Weekend is now complimented by an Art Week in September that bundles art berlin contemporary, Premium art fair and other initiatives. The three major institutions for contemporary art have access to a small municipal budget to present the local art production that was spent on Based in Berlin, but they remain underfinanced and staffed with local directors, which limits their international reach.[10] Nonetheless a self-confident art scene positions itself as an influential actor, both for urban development and as a generator of economic growth. Without international spending power and public funding, it relies on numerous – often solitary – private initiatives.

To live in the myth of Berlin in 2012 is, in reality, to range from naïve self-delusion to enthusiastic confidence about taking part in what is said to be one of the world's most promising art centres.

1   Isabelle Graw 'Ein Schaufenster in Berlin. Anmerkungen zum Wert der (vermeintlichen) Marktferne', Becker, Conny *et. al.* [ed.]: *Metropolitan Views: Berlin*, Berlin. Kunstszenen 1989 – 2009

2   cf. Kulturwirtschaftsbericht 2008

3   cf. Timm, Tobias 'Berlin, der schönste Kunstspielplatz der Welt', in: *ZEIT ONLINE*, 07.06.2011

4   The privately initiated 'Temporäre Kunsthalle' in 2008 / 2009 was a failure due to factionalism, debatable programming and lack of public interest. The urge among artists, curators, critics to obtain more exhibition space to present the latest of artistic production was shared by neither the population of Berlin nor the thousands of tourists coming every year – even after entry was made free.

5   €600,000: province budget granted in 2009; €1,000,000: donation by Lotto Foundation – presided over by the mayor of Berlin, Klaus Wowereit.

6   cf. Timm 2011; Williams, Gisela 'Despite Criticism, Berlin Art Festival Arrives', the *New York Times*, 03.06.2011

7   According to the manifesto of the initiative 'to have and to need', no more than 8% of Berlin based artists have a permanent relationship with a gallery. No more than a third of these galleries are located in Berlin. Manifest. Haben und Brauchen

8   cf. Kito Nedo 'Berlin entmachtet sich', *Berliner Zeitung*, 12.07.2012

9   tagesspiegel.de/kultur/querelen-um-postfuhramt-keine-loesung-fuer-c-o-berlin/7075518.html

10 Becker, Conny/Landbrecht, Christina: 'Alle Lechzen nach Aufmerksamkeit – und finden sie immer weniger. Interview mit Jörg Heiser', Becker, Conny *et. al.* [ed.]: *Metropolitan Views: Berlin*, Berlin. Kunstszenen 1989 – 2009

To Have and to Need
Fact Sheet

Artist income[1]

◩ I produce little to no income

▦ I produce an income, but it doesn't cover living expenses

▨ My income is sufficient for a modest lifestyle

▥ My income is very good

◪ No response

To Have and to Need

In response to the worsening work and living conditions for artists in Berlin, an informal circle of individuals working in art was formed in 2010, in order to address the recurring issues regarding cultural and urban politics in the city. The project was called *Haben und Brauchen* ('to have and to need') and was designed as a platform for discussion and action in order to preserve artistic freedom and diversity.

Their first action was an open letter addressed to Klaus Wowereit, Mayor of Berlin, in January 2011 in response to the planning of the *Leistungsschau junger Kunst in Berlin* ('Achievement Show of Young Berlin Art'), a governmentally conceived and funded art exhibition for the following summer.

The letter criticised the neoliberal rhetoric and aim of the project and accused it of exploiting artists for the city's branding and marketing without offering anything in return. It addressed the declining living conditions of artists and the lack of funding and called for a boycott of the *Leistungsschau*.

In January 2012, the collective decided to elaborate their aims and demands more clearly by publishing a manifesto called 'to have and to need', in which they criticised the lack of support by the local government in light of its contradictory glorification of the Berlin art scene. They called for the preservation of the conditions that allow artists to pursue their craft, and hoped to re-launch the discussion of the effects of gentrification. In their own words, they compared the creative class to 'one-armed patients who have learned the initiative to self-dependently bind their own wounds.'[2]

Finally, they emphasise the value of art as separate from economic values, and to recognise artistic activities as work and remunerate it accordingly. Contrary to neoliberal beliefs, the art market alone cannot regulate and preserve the qualities of Berlin's art scene and the city government is urged to take responsibility. Artists are demanding their fair share of the improvements and commercial revenue their activities bring to the city.

Written and researched by Henrike Dessaules

1   Kultur - und Kreativwirtschaftsindex Berlin – Brandenburg 2011: Wirtschaftliche Stimmung und Standortbewertung (Ergebnisbericht), Berlin 2011

2   To have and to need (Haben und Brauchen) – Manifesto, *habenundbrauchen.de*, Berlin 2012, p. 3.

Hannah Höch and the First Mythos Berlin
Daniel Herrmann

154 – 158

Starting with a Bang: Hannah Höch and the First International Dada Fair, Berlin 1920

A spectre was haunting the Lützow-Ufer – the spectre of Dadaism. It hung from the ceiling and peered down from the walls, it sat on pedestals and screamed from posters: 'TAKE DADA SERIOUSLY' – only to add, winking slighting at the visitor, 'it's worth it.' From 30 June to 25 August 1920, the Kunsthandlung Dr Otto Burchard, an art gallery near the bustling Potsdamer Platz and close to the lush Tiergarten, had been turned into the venue for the First International Dada Fair, and it promised revolution.

Even its bold invitation card took a fervent stance in the Weimar Republic's post-war capital:

> 'The Dadaistic person is the radical opponent of exploitation; the logic of exploitation creates nothing but fools, and the Dadaistic person hates stupidity and loves nonsense! Thus, the Dadaistic person shows himself to be truly real, as opposed to the stinking hypocrisy of the patriarch and to the capitalist perishing in his armchair.' [1]

The exclamatory mood prevailed inside the fairly small venue. In a mockery of an academic, salon-style exhibition, its walls were covered with large typographic posters, small frames with photomontages, with cut-outs and expansive paintings that used traditional oils as much as rough materials, looking like they were picked up from the gutter which the painting depicted. Collage, montage, and found images were the common denominators in the cacophony of carnivalistic commands hurled at the spectator: 'Finally open up your mind!' screamed one large photographic poster, 'Against Art!' another. From the ceiling hung what looked like a horrible mannequin – a human shape with a pig's mask stuffed into a German military uniform, looming grotesquely over artworks and visitors alike.

Artists Raoul Hausmann (1886 – 1971) and Hannah Höch (1889 – 1978) at the Internation Dada Fair, Berlin in 1920. Photo by Apic / Getty Images

The artist list of the Dada Fair reads like a who's-who of the Berlin Dada art world in the 1920s: Jean Arp, Johannes Baader, Otto Dix, Max Ernst, George Grosz, Raoul Hausmann, Wieland Herzfelde and many other now famous figures of European art history all contributed to the exhibition. Hausmann, famous agitator and polemicist, had penned the invitation's pointed manifesto; Dix had sent paintings certain to antagonise traditional taste; Grosz played a central role in organising the event and Herzfelde contributed significantly to the exhibition's catalogue. Their's was a rambunctious, chest-beating, clamorous affair, and it was supposed to be. In the First International Dada Fair, the 'Roaring Twenties' roared with a vengeance, straight into the face of any visitor. Exhibiting artists asserted their opposition to the traditional tastes, artistic media, and forms of organisation left over from Imperial Germany, and they did not do this quietly.

Instead of breathing 'a soul' into the representations of reality as they saw to be the Impressionists' want, or 'endlessly presenting nothing but the world within their own breasts', as they accused the Expressionists of doing,[2] the Dadaists set out to embrace the fragmented noise of the city, the turmoil of the vast political change of their time, and the huge increase in imagery which photography in the age of mass-reproduction was producing. Shattering artistic conventions of the past, the First International Dada Fair celebrated the triumph of the cut-and-paste of pieces, of collage: instead of the traditional paint and brush, the Dadaists declared they would take up 'scissors and cut out all that we require from paintings and photographic representations.'[3]

The artwork that perhaps most succinctly exemplified the spirit, the medium and the political bite of its tumultuous time was 'Cut with the Kitchen Knife Dada through the Last Weimar Beer-Belly Cultural Epoch of Germany'. A sizeable collage, its several layers of cut-outs confronted images from mass-culture, politics and engineering with advertising language, disjointed newspaper headlines, fashion photographs and architectural vistas. Visitors could make out the pensive face of Albert Einstein, the social-democratic politician Friedrich Ebert seemingly sprouting from his temple; they would find the artist Käthe Kollwitz; the de-throned Kaiser, his famous moustache ridiculously formed by the bodies of two handsome wrestlers. The heads of fellow artists were transplanted onto the bodies of babies, sculptures or deep diving suits. Over and over, the images of dancers and the mixing of gender conventions play a powerfully comic role, gaudily displaying the head of the right-wing Field Marshall Hindenburg on the body of a scantily clad female dancer,

Hannah Höch and the First Mythos Berlin

or showing the popular dancer Niddy Impekoven perform-
ing on the bald head of the politician Walther Rathenau.
Juxtaposing images, the work created new, mischievous
narratives. Elevating sources from popular culture and mass
production, from the flotsam and jetsam of current affairs
to the stage of an art exhibition, it was sure to draw criticism
from traditionalists. The work was large, it was striking,
it wielded satire like a weapon. And, amidst the sound and
the fury from the brash and brazen bunch of boisterous
blokes who made up the Berlin Dadaists, it was made by
a woman.

Hannah Höch, born 1889, had been an active member of
the Berlin avant-garde for several years. Having escaped the
education traditional to women of her generation by moving
from provincial Thuringia to the cosmopolitan Berlin and
enrolling in the School of Applied Arts, Höch soon made
contact with the 'Der Sturm' Gallery and its circle of influential artists. With initiative and genuine curiosity, Höch met
performers, artists, sepulchral architects and philosophers;
she enrolled in calligrapy and life drawing classes, executed
wood engravings for her teachers and published her own
woodcuts. She also found employment at one of the foremost
German publishing houses for fashion and photo journalism, the Ullstein Verlag, designing patterns and writing for
its popular women's publications. Right at the centre of this
nascent, exciting and quickly expanding form of journalism,
her fascination with extant imagery soon met the rebellious
spirit of the Dada movement: 'Already before the end of the
war, in 1918, young people in Berlin had become politically
rebellious and were also looking for new intellectual
options... [Dada and its Swiss harbinger Richard Huelsenbeck]

acted in Berlin like a match, lighting up a powder keg. Dada exploded.'[4]

Holding her artistic own in a crowd of mainly young men, Höch published, produced and exhibited in Dada magazines, at Dada events and in Dada exhibitions. The most important of these was the First International Dada Fair. The work of Hannah Höch was considered among the best of the exhibition but, more than anything, the spirit and the artistic means of the movement that she was part of were considered indicative of a generation. At the beginning of the decade that inter-war Berlin was to become so famous for, 'the art of the Dadaists can only be immediate expression of our own time. It can hardly be different from the Today. [The architect, author and German proponent of the English Arts and Crafts movement, Hermann Muthesius] recently wrote the darling sentence, "Art can transport people to a better place". That is a typically bourgeois idea. Dada shows the world as it is in 1920.'[5]

---

1   Raoul Hausmann, Invitation Card to the First International Dada Fair, Berlin 1920. Translated in: Wieland Herzfelde and Bridget Doherty, 'Introduction to the First International Dada Fair', *October*, vol. 105, (Summer 2003), p. 96.

2   Wieland Herzfelde in the introduction to the exhibition catalogue, translated in: Herzfelde & Doherty, as footnote 1, p. 101.

3   *ibid.*

4   Hannah Höch, 'Lebensrückblick 1958', in: *Hannah Höch. Ihr Werk – Ihr Leben – Ihre Freunde.* Exhib.-Cat. Berlinische Galerie, Berlin 1989, pp. 1958.

5   Adolf Behne, 'Dada', Exhibition Review, in: *Die Freiheit*, July 9 1920, Evening Edition.

Hannah Höch and the First Mythos Berlin

Interview with Jessica Morgan
Sarah Hegenbart

160 – 162

SARAH HEGENBART

What do you think distinguishes Berlin from other art centres?

JESSICA MORGAN

This very much depends upon which lens you use to observe the city. Your focus is the artistic community of the city, though even this is difficult to summarise. As an outsider, the city has a relaxed (at times even lazy?) ambience that is unlike other cosmopolitan areas of Germany and indeed most European cities. Though this statement should be qualified by the differing realities of West and East Berlin. To my eyes there is at times an artificiality to Berlin: a performed presence, as if everyone who is there has chosen (for this moment at least) to join in the staging of a relaxed 'new-bohemia'.

SARAH HEGENBART

What are the main differences between Berlin and London?

JESSICA MORGAN

The economic imperatives of London are a constant presence and it is a city driven by commercial interest. Berlin still allows for an existence that is not exclusively commandeered by this type of energy and self-interest.

SARAH HEGENBART

Who is your favourite Berlin-based artist?

JESSICA MORGAN

Of the artists based there that I meet, work and talk with, Tino Sehgal and Anri Sala would probably be the most significant in recent years.

Interview with Jessica Morgan

SARAH HEGENBART

How do you explain the near-mythical status that Berlin exerts on contemporary art practice?

JESSICA MORGAN

I think this needs to be placed in perspective. I am not sure Berlin holds this status outside of Europe. Certainly, it would take a great deal to convince New York of its secondary status to any city. In the global art world I think its significance is only as a temporary learning / stopping ground not as a site of long term production and inspiration. For every artist who has stayed after temporarily making a home in Berlin there are many more who have left. What has generated this impression though is the combination of the lack of urgency in the city which allows for a type of relaxed interaction and the DAAD which has almost single handedly been responsible for bringing artists to Berlin for lengthy periods of time.

SARAH HEGENBART

Which cities do you personally view as most exciting for emerging young artists?

JESSICA MORGAN

Mexico City has proved to be a very productive place, as well as São Paulo and Rio de Janeiro. Istanbul and Beirut are both very engaged places to be with an increasing number of support structures for artists. New York is perpetually exciting no matter how much one may wish to ignore it and Los Angeles and Vancouver have a particular teaching-based community of artists which results in close ties and affiliations as well as support.

SARAH HEGENBART

How can a move to another city affect artistic practice? Could you mention an example of a contemporary artist whose move to another city resulted in a shift in his work?

JESSICA MORGAN

I suppose there are always issues of scale and access that cities can provide and a community of fellow artists or intellects. But I would be suspicious of an artist who completely changed track because of these influences.

SARAH HEGENBART

To what extent do the easier living conditions (lower rents, bigger studio space etc.) in Berlin affect artistic practice?

JESSICA MORGAN

It is almost entirely the reason why artists stay. How it affects practice is by allowing a practice to happen, though perhaps one might argue that it allows too many people to practice who shouldn't.

SARAH HEGENBART

One suggestion is that 'existential pressure' as artists face it in London rather than in Berlin can be inspiring. Do you agree with this?

JESSICA MORGAN

Different artists are inspired by different states of being.

Interview with Jessica Morgan

Biographies

Hannah Arnold was born in Göttingen in 1988. She is currently reading for a DPhil at Oxford, examining the influence of German literature on W. H. Auden. Additionally she works as a freelance editor, translator and German tutor and has recently inherited the literary journal TEXT + KRITIK from her father.

Aeneas Bastian was born in Berlin in 1975. He lives and works in the city as a gallerist and author.

In 2009 **Katharina Beckmann** (Heritage Conservation & Architecture), **Stefanie Gerke** & **Nele Heinevetter** (Art History) founded NICHE BERLIN to open up new Berlin perspectives for art and architecture lovers from all over the world.

Samara Grace Chadwick was raised on a farm on the Canadian east coast, and later spent many years as a would-be Berliner. She is now writing a thesis in Cultural Studies within the Erasmus Mundus Joint Doctorate programme in Literary Interzones and lives in Rio de Janeiro.

Dr Richard Cork is an art critic, historian, broadcaster and curator.

Christina Danick studied cultural studies in Hildesheim and Paris. She is currently enrolled at Humboldt University of Berlin, finishing her master's degree.

Susanna Davies-Crook is an artist and writer based in Berlin and London. She is a contributing editor for

Dazed & Confused and the Berlin-based *Sleek Magazine*, and art editor for *Exberliner*.

Henrike Dessaules is the author of the blog Discipline and Anarchy. disciplineandanarchy.com

Donatien Grau is a contributing editor of *Flash Art International*.

Sarah Günther recently completed her MA in Comparative Politics at the London School of Economics and Political Science. She was born in Potsdam, Germany.

Daniel Herrmann is the curatorial programme manager at the Whitechapel Gallery, London. He was previously curator of the Paolozzi Collection and 20th-century works on paper at the Scottish National Gallery of Modern Art, Edinburgh.

Rye Dag Holmboe is a writer and PhD candidate who lives in London. He recently edited the book *Existere*.

John Holten is a novelist, editor and curator. His critically-acclaimed novel *The Readymades* was published in 2011 by Broken Dimanche Press. Born in Ireland, he now lives in Berlin. johnholten.com

Katie Paterson's conceptual projects make use of sophisticated technologies and specialist expertise to stage intimate, poetic and philosophical engagements between people and their natural environment.

Robert Rapoport is currently completing his PhD at Oxford University. His films have shown at festivals across the UK and Germany. He recently won awards at the Oxford Film Festival for Best Film (2010) and Best Cinematography (2012). robertrapoport.com

Martina Schmücker currently lives and works in London. She also teaches as a visiting tutor at the Ruskin School of Drawing and Fine Art in Oxford. She lived in Berlin from 1997 until 2003, when she came to London to study at the Royal College of Art.

Vid Simoniti was born in Ljubljana, Slovenia. He holds a BPhil in Philosophy and is currently writing his doctoral thesis at the Ruskin School of Drawing and Fine Art, University of Oxford. He co-curated the recent exhibition 'In-Site: Art as a Mode of Enquiry' at the Ashmolean Museum, and writes regularly for *Pogledi* magazine in Slovenia.

Daniel Udy is currently studying for his BFA in Fine Art at the Ruskin School of Drawing & Fine Art, University of Oxford. His research interests are focused on intersections between art and politics in late postmodernism, and upcoming publications include *The Edgware Road: A Socio-Cultural History*, published via Serpentine Gallery.

The exhibition *Mythos Berlin*, curated by Sarah Hegenbart and Sven Mündner, opened at the German Embassy London on 10 October 2012. It featured work by: Erin Hughes & Jennifer Mustapha; Nick Jeffrey; Jan Kaesbach; Julia Prezewowsky; Robert Rapoport; Viktor Timofeev and Daniel Udy.

MYTHOS BERLIN
a London Perspective

Editors: Sarah Hegenbart, Sven Mündner, Benjamin Eastham
Assistant Editor: Mary Hannity
Design and cover art: Ken Kirton
Picture Editor: Octavia Lamb

With our sincere thanks to His Excellency the German Ambassador to the Court of St James, Georg Boomgaarden.

We would also like to extend our gratitude to: Christian Boros, Sadie Coles, Christina Danick, Henrike Dessaules, Olafur Eliasson, Jason Gaiger, Andreas Gegner, Sarah Günther, John Hyman, Cord Meier-Klodt, Fabian Knecht, Holger Königsdörfer, Dörte Mang, Jessica Morgan, Jost Münster, Ruskin School of Drawing & Fine Art Oxford, Annette Schryen, Paolo Stolpmann, Wolfgang Tillmans, Universität der Künste Berlin, Johann Voss, Margaretha Weber.

Printed by PUSH, London on Olin regular cream from Antalis McNaughton and Hello gloss from Robert Horne. Set in Acon courtesy of Holger Königsdörfer and Oops Grotesque courtesy of the designer of the publication.

Published by The White Review
Edition of 1,000
ISBN 978-0-9568001-5-2
© German Embassy London and Individual Contributors, 2012.

The White Review, 1 Knightsbridge Green, London SW1X 7QA.
The White Review is a registered charity in the United Kingdom, Charity Number 1148690

mythosberlin.net

October 2012